sandra lee
Semi-Homemade®

miramax books

HYPERION

New York

ISBN 1-4013-5923-X

First Paperback Edition
10 9 8 7 6 5 4 3 2

sandra lee
Semi-Homemade® Cooking

Quick Marvelous Meals and Nothing Is Made from Scratch

acknowledgements

THE TEAM

Maryellen Baker, Ed Ouellette and Joe Buissink: *Photographers*; Hilary Hollingshead: *Layout*

Norman Stewart and DoHan Rogers: *Food Stylists*; Kathy Talley-Jones: *Indexer*

Jonathan Burnham, Kathy Schneider, Hilary Bass and Kristin Powers: *Publishing Team*

Rochelle Palermo Torres: *Semi-Homemade Recipe Tester*
Ms. Palermo began her career in food writing at *Bon Appétit* magazine, and currently serves as an ongoing contributor. Her responsibilities have included the testing and editing of recipes for such world-renowned chefs as Lorenzo di Medici, Thomas Keller, and Emeril Lagasse. Ms. Palermo created, produced, and wrote the successful newsletter "Food for Thought" for Cooking.com and recently completed 120 recipes for the cookbook created by Ludovic Lefebvre, L'Orangerie's executive chef.

Lane Crowther: *Semi-Homemade Recipe and Wine Editor*
Lane Crowther, educated at the acclaimed Cordon Bleu, is a cookbook author, recipe developer, and food stylist. Throughout her culinary career wine has been a dominant factor for her when developing recipes. Ms. Crowther owns a Pinot Noir producing vineyard in the Williamette Valley. She currently develops recipes and styles the "Cooking Class" feature as a contributing editor for *Bon Appétit* magazine, and previously served as the *Bon Appétit* director of the Recipe-Testing Program.

Denise Vivaldo: *Semi-Homemade Food Stylist*
Beginning her culinary training at the Ritz Escoffier and La Varenne, Paris, Ms. Vivaldo graduated Chef de Cuisine from the California Culinary Academy in 1984. Her expert food preparation and event planning have been commissioned by *Sunset* magazine; *Los Angeles* magazine; and *People* magazine, for their Celebrity Chef series. Ms. Vivaldo also has served as a creative consultant, recipe developer, and food stylist for many popular chefs and nationally recognized fitness gurus, including Wolfgang Puck, Julia Child, Suzanne Somers, and Richard Simmons.

Brenda Koplin: *Semi-Homemade Copy Editor*
Brenda Koplin has a Bachelor of Arts in Journalism and served as the copy chief of *Bon Appétit* magazine for over sixteen years. Currently Ms. Koplin is a freelance copy editor for a variety of food and cooking publications. Her most recent work includes copy editing for the *Hot Sauce Bible* and the *El Cholo Restaurant Cookbook*.

DEDICATION

This book is dedicated to my grandmother,
Lorraine Korth Waldroop,
whose love and guidance made me the person I am.
How fortunate I was to have you.
s.l.

SPECIAL THANKS

Bruce Karatz, my husband, for your commitment, devotion and love

Peggy and Bill Singlehurst, my aunt and uncle, for all your love and support

Kimber Lee, my sister, who's always been there for me or gone there for me, I love you

Cynthia Christi-Lee, my sister, for sharing your most precious creations so unselfishly

Rich and Paul (Johnny) Christiansen, my brothers, I'm so proud of you both

Lee Gaskill and Michele Christiansen, for being such wonderful additions to our family

Scottie, Danielle, Brandon, Austen, Stephanie, Taner, Bryce, and Blake,
my nieces and nephews, who are sweeter than any dessert I could ever make

Aspen, my baby dog, who owns my heart and is the inspiration behind the Pet Foods chapter

Colleen Schmidt, my best friend, for all the corn dogs, root beer floats, dreams, and confidences

Zane Rothschild, my mentor, whose little nudges along the way help me choose the right paths

Linda Willemse and Linda Tobin, my assistants, whose help and devotion
make it possible for me to do what I do

Barbara Guggenheim, Bert Fields, Tina Brown, Harvey Weinstein, Bob Weinstein, Wolfgang Puck,
Mary Sugarman, Dick Clark, Harvey Mackay, Charles Layton, and Steve Hutensky,
who have inspired me and advised me — thank you

TABLE OF CONTENTS

Table of Contents

INTRODUCTION FROM WOLFGANG PUCK

As a chef, one of the comments I hear most often from my customers is that they don't have enough time to cook at home anymore. That's why I'm so happy to see that my friend Sandra Lee has come up with her own unique solution to that problem.

Sandra starts with a wide assortment of convenience foods that you can find in any supermarket—preshredded carrots, bottled lemon juice, frozen puff pastry, fresh pastas, pregrated cheeses, canned soups and sauces, boxed cake and pudding mixes, and more. She puts these everyday ingredients together, adds a generous measure of her own talent, creativity, and flair, and the results are astonishing. Not only do her recipes look good, but they taste delicious too.

While I have many sous chefs in my restaurants, chopping, dicing, making stocks, mixing doughs, and so on, Sandra puts the entire American food industry to work for you. So, no matter how busy you are, in Sandra's book you will always find delicious-tasting shortcuts. Her "Semi-Homemade" approach will help bring you, your family, and friends back into the kitchen and to the dinner table, no matter how busy you may be.

Sandra's approach to cooking is filled with a sense of fun and a love of sharing good food with others. Her enthusiasm is contagious, and her warm personality shines from every page of this book.

Live, love, eat...and have the time to enjoy it all!

Wolfgang Puck

LETTER FROM SANDRA

Semi-Homemade Cooking will make your life much easier than it's ever been before! I've spent the past ten years creating a Semi-Homemade lifestyle for myself—and now for you—busy people on a budget and on the go. Our days are filled with too much to do, too little time to do it in, and not enough money to make it all happen. Life today requires us all to be super-human. "To-do" lists have gone from one-page handwritten sheets to entire chapters in a hardbound book. And after getting all your "to-dos" done, you're expected to plan, shop for, and whip up new, fresh, mouth-watering homemade meals from scratch?

What is Semi-Homemade cooking? It's a new way of cooking where nothing is made from scratch. The Semi-Homemade cooking approach is easily done by combining several prepackaged foods, a few fresh ingredients, and a "pinch of this with a hint of that" to make new, easy, gourmet-tasting, inexpensive meals in minutes. It's fast, fabulous food.

How will *Semi-Homemade Cooking* make your life easier? Each recipe comes complete with time estimates for planning, cost guidelines for budgeting, and a suggested brand-name list of ingredients to ease your shopping load. So whether you are cooking for two or twenty, there will always be something easy, quick, and affordable to prepare. You'll be the "Julia Child" of your own kitchen without the time, energy, and expense it normally requires.

What will you get here that you can't get anywhere else? You'll get an entirely new way of cooking. You'll get recipes complete with actual brand names of products to use so you can be sure the recipe you create tastes exactly like it should, every time. You'll get the benefit of quality and taste without the stress traditional cooking creates.

I'd love to hear your thoughts, ideas, questions, or suggestions. I've included a prepaid postage card, my address, and e-mail for your convenience (see page 204). Welcome to the new Semi-Homemade world!

Sandra Lee

GROCERY SHOPPING

Grocery shopping can be made so much easier by including the following helpful hints and timesaving tricks into your weekly routine:

Plan your entire week's menu in advance. This takes a bit of effort, but is sure to help you avoid stress later.

Try to do all your shopping on one day and stay away from shopping at peak hours.

Getting in and out of the grocery store can be much quicker if you create a shopping list and organize it by categories such as packaged goods, baked goods, canned and jarred products, produce, meats, dairy, frozen foods, household products, and cleaning items. Creating this aisle-by-aisle shopping guide will surely make you more efficient.

It's best to load your cart with nonperishables first, followed by produce, dairy products, meats and seafood, then finish up with frozen foods on top.

Check the dates of all perishable items. Purchase containers that have the longest indicated dates of expiration.

Purchase produce that is just ripe, or almost ripe, based on when they will be served (advance weekly menus come in handy here). Be careful when purchasing fully ripe or over-ripe produce, it can go bad instantly.

Saving money can be simpler than you think. By clipping just a couple of coupons and signing up for free membership discount cards, given at most larger grocery store chains, you're sure to save a surprising sum.

Get your groceries home and into the refrigerator or freezer quickly. If you plan on doing other errands before going home, bring along a thermal cooler to keep chilled foods cool.

Try not to shop on an empty stomach. When hungry, you're more likely to make impulse purchases, spending more money and time than you anticipated. If you're famished, visit the bakery or deli department for a quick fix before shopping.

DISPOSABLES

Making life easier can be so simple if you utilize disposable products. Paper plates, napkins, plastic utensils, baking dishes, serving bowls and platters are all readily available. Disposable items provide quick preparation and cleanup— you'll minimize your work while maximizing your leisure time.

BRAND NAMES

Stylish, quality cooking is made easy when using our suggestions for preselected and tested name-brand foods. These precombined ingredient sources reduce expenses and enhance taste. Substitutions, of course, are always at your discretion. Brand-name suggestions are highlighted in italics throughout each recipe and are available through most major grocery store chains.

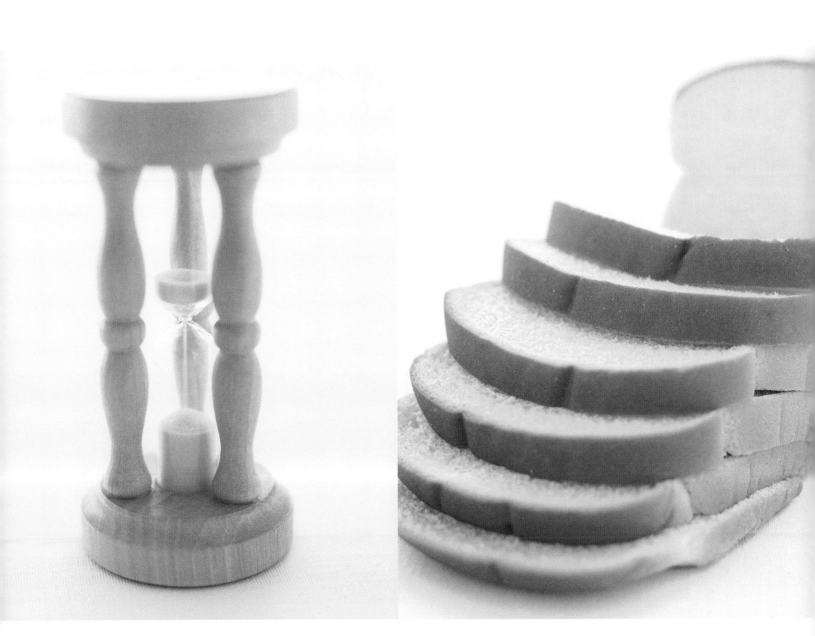

PREPPING, COOKING, AND COOLING TIMES

Time is on your side. Each quick, easy recipe comes complete with time estimates for prepping, cooking, and cooling. You decide how much time you want to spend in your kitchen: a new luxury you're sure to utilize, appreciate, and enjoy.

BUDGET

Even when on a budget, there is no need to sacrifice the quality or quantity of your food. With so much to choose from in all price ranges, budgets can be easy to accommodate with a little know-how. The $ signs shown with each recipe give you a guideline of the cost per serving.

Inexpensive	$	Low Cost	$$
Medium Cost	$$$	Expensive	$$$$

LEFTOVERS

Food can be even more delicious the second time around. When stored properly and reheated slowly, food frequently tends to taste better with time. Reheatable leftovers should be placed in shallow storage containers, which allow food to cool or reheat quickly. Recipes that make great leftovers are noted with instructions for serving a second time.

STORAGE

Reusable plastic storage containers are convenient, airtight, and lock in freshness and guarantee food lasts longer. They are perfect to use in the pantry, refrigerator, and freezer. Be sure to mark with contents and date. Store do-ahead dinners and leftovers in shallow containers. See simple storage suggestions that accompany many recipes.

M U S I C

Music sets a mood and creates ambience. It can mellow you out, lift you up, or get you going. It can remind you of past memories, or create new ones. Music selections are shared in most of the chapters. So throughout your busy day, remember to "hear the music."

WINES

A good wine, whether expensive or not, warms the way to ending the day. It's a palate-pleaser before, during, or after dinner and a relaxing way to enjoy a weekend lunch or an afternoon brunch. Try the suggested wines and soon you, too, will feel as knowledgeable as any connoisseur.

BREAKFAST

Breakfast, as they say, is the most important meal of the day. This may be true, but try to convince yourself to sit down for five minutes and eat when you're running late, not hungry, and can't even see straight, much less make breakfast. Growing up, I was fine with Cap'n Crunch® and milk—that much sugar will give anyone plenty of energy…for a while. But the nutritional value, or lack thereof, will send your energy crashing way before lunchtime. Still, I must admit, a sugar-filled breakfast of Cap'n Crunch® is better than no breakfast at all.

Without breakfast, you feel exhausted even after a great night's sleep. You find yourself becoming easily irritable and having difficulty concentrating. A bad morning, or even a bad day, cannot always be blamed on waking up on the wrong side of the bed. Rather, it's trying to function properly and at full capacity without giving your body what it needs: fuel.

This chapter is filled with delicious, simple breakfast choices that will jump-start your day. Some are sugar-filled (because I couldn't resist), and most can be prepared the night before and reheated the next day to make your precious morning moments even more manageable.

Breakfast

CREPES BENEDICT

Serves 2

4	slices turkey bacon, *Butterball®*
2	10-inch prepared crepes, *Mrs. Frieda®*
4	eggs
2	tablespoons butter, *Land O'Lakes®*
1	can (4-ounce) hollandaise sauce, *Aunt Penny's®*
	Salt and pepper

Prep time: 2 minutes
Cooking time: 8 minutes

Preparation:

Prepare bacon according to package instructions.
Place crepes in plastic wrap and heat in microwave on high for 20 seconds.
Whisk eggs in a bowl.
Over medium heat, melt butter in a medium skillet.
Add eggs and stir constantly until light and fluffy, about 2 minutes.
Season eggs to taste with salt and pepper.
Place hollandaise sauce in a cup and microwave on high for about 45 seconds,
    stirring every 15 seconds.
Season sauce to taste with salt and pepper. Set aside.
Place 1 crepe on each breakfast plate.
Spoon half the scrambled eggs into the center of each crepe and top with 2 bacon slices.
Roll up enchilada-style.
Top with 3 tablespoons of hollandaise sauce and serve.

$$

Music: *Natalie MacMaster, "In My Hands"*

FRENCH APPLE-RAISIN SANDWICHES

French toast has always been one of my favorite breakfasts. This recipe is especially good because the bread becomes perfectly crunchy around the edges and mildly toasty through the center, while the apple filling adds a soft and sweet accompaniment. Adding syrup makes this breakfast truly decadent.

Serves 2

2   eggs
1/4 cup whole milk
1/4 teaspoon ground cinnamon, *McCormick®*
4   slices raisin bread, *Wonder®*
1/2 cup prepared apple pie filling, *Comstock®*
1   tablespoon butter, *Land O'Lakes®*
    Additional butter
    Confectioners/powdered sugar (optional)

Prep time: 5 minutes
Cooking time: 8 minutes

Preparation:

In a large baking dish, whisk eggs, milk, and cinnamon. Set aside.
Make 2 sandwiches with the bread and apple pie filling.
Place sandwiches in egg mixture.
Let soak until egg mixture is completely absorbed into the bread, turning sandwiches over occasionally, about 3 minutes.
On a griddle over medium low heat, melt 1 tablespoon of butter.
Cook sandwiches on the griddle until brown and heated through, about 4 minutes per side.
Cut each sandwich in half.
Transfer to plates and serve with additional butter. Top with confectioners/powdered sugar (optional).

$$

Music: *Dori Caymmi, Self-Titled*

HUEVOS RANCHEROS

This is my all-time favorite breakfast. My nephew Scottie and I have a great time making it and we always use a fun cookie cutter shape to cut the tortillas, such as a coyote, cactus, or cowboy hat.

Serves 4

4	burrito-size flour tortillas, *Mission®*
1	can (16-ounce) low-fat refried black beans, *Rosarita®*
2	tablespoons diced green chiles, *Ortega®*
1/2	cup salsa, *Pace®*
2	tablespoons fresh cilantro, chopped
8	eggs
1/4	cup shredded sharp cheddar cheese, *Kraft®*
2	green onions, thinly sliced
4	tablespoons sour cream

Prep time: 5 minutes
Cooking time: 12 minutes

Preparation:

Preheat oven to 400 degrees.
Cut tortillas into shapes using cookie cutters and place on a foil-covered baking sheet.
Bake until slightly browned, about 4 minutes per side.
Meanwhile, combine beans, green chiles, salsa, and cilantro in a medium saucepan.
Bring to a simmer over medium heat, stirring occasionally, about 4 minutes.
Remove from heat.
Cook eggs over easy or sunny-side up.
Divide bean mixture among 4 plates.
Place 2 cooked eggs next to the beans on each plate.
Arrange the baked tortillas in beans and sprinkle with cheese and green onions.
Top with a dollop of sour cream and serve.

$ Music: *Loreena McKennit, "The Book of Secrets"*

MORNING GLORY FONDUE

This fondue is fabulous! I get so many compliments on this breakfast. It's truly original and quite delicious—an interesting new take on an old favorite. If you're serving it as a dish for a weekend brunch, place it at the center of your table to be presented as the focal point of the meal—it's that special.

Serves 6

2	packages (8 ounces each) cream cheese, *Philadelphia®*
1	cup sour cream
2	tablespoons all-purpose flour, *Pillsbury®*
1	tablespoon Dijon mustard, *French's®*
1	cup brut champagne, *Cook's®*
6	ounces smoked salmon, chopped, *Lasco®*
10	cherry tomatoes, quartered
4	hard-boiled eggs, peeled and coarsely chopped
6	English muffins, toasted and cut into 1-inch pieces, *Thomas'®*
3	bagels (plain, water, or egg), halved lengthwise, cut into 1-inch pieces, toasted

Prep time: 7 minutes
Cooking time: 8 minutes

Preparation:

In a large bowl, using an electric mixer, beat the cream cheese, sour cream, flour, and
  mustard until well blended.
Bring champagne to a boil in a heavy medium saucepan over medium high heat.
Reduce heat to medium low.
Gradually whisk cheese mixture into champagne, stirring until cheese melts and
  mixture is smooth.
Stir in salmon, tomatoes, and eggs.
Transfer fondue to fondue pot or bowl and keep warm.
Serve hot with warmed English muffins and bagel pieces for dipping, speared on forks.

$$ Music: *Passion Planet, Various Artists, "Songs of Love from Around the World"*

PUMPKIN CINNAMON PANCAKES

If you're a pumpkin lover like me, I've got your number—six that is! This stack of six pancakes is every pumpkin fan's dream. I got this idea on a fall trip to New York. It was "pumpkin everything" at the Regency Hotel, and the pumpkin pancakes were the best I'd ever had—so here's my Semi-Homemade version for you to enjoy! I'd love to hear what you think. (See page 204.)

Serves 2

PECAN SYRUP:
1   cup maple flavored pancake syrup, *Log Cabin Original Syrup®*
5   tablespoons pecans, toasted and chopped, *Diamond®*

PANCAKES:
1   cup buttermilk pancake mix, *Aunt Jemima®*
2/3   cup cold water
1/3   cup canned pumpkin, *Libby's®*
1/2   teaspoon ground cinnamon, *McCormick®*
1/8   teaspoon ground ginger, *McCormick®*
       Nonstick vegetable cooking spray, *PAM®*
       Butter, room temperature, *Land O'Lakes®*

Prep time: 5 minutes
Cooking time: 6 minutes

Pecan Syrup Preparation:

Combine maple syrup and pecans in small microwave-safe bowl.
Heat in microwave on high until hot, about 25 seconds.
Set pecan syrup aside and keep warm.

Pancake Preparation:

In a medium bowl, whisk pancake mix, water, pumpkin, cinnamon, and ginger until just
   blended (do not overmix; mixture should be lumpy).
Spray a heavy griddle with nonstick spray and heat griddle over medium heat.
Spoon 2 tablespoons of batter onto griddle to form each pancake.
Cook for 2 minutes or until bubbles appear, then turn pancakes over and cook for
   2 minutes longer.
Transfer pancakes to plates.
Top with butter and serve with warm pecan syrup.

$$ Music: *Ella Fitzgerald, "Priceless Jazz Collection"*

ENGLISH CROWN SCRAMBLE

Serves 6

MORNAY SAUCE:
2	tablespoons butter, *Land O'Lakes®*
1 1/2	tablespoons all-purpose flour, *Pillsbury®*
1 1/4	cups whole milk
1/4	teaspoon salt
3/4	cup shredded Swiss cheese, *Sargento®*
1/2	cup shredded Parmesan cheese, *Kraft®*

EGG PASTRY CROWNS:
6	frozen puff pastry shells, *Pepperidge Farm®*
6	eggs, slightly beaten
1/4	cup whole milk
1	teaspoon vegetable oil, *Wesson®*
1	tablespoon butter, *Land O'Lakes®*
	Salt and pepper
2	tablespoons fresh chives, chopped

Prep time:	5 minutes
Cooking time:	15 minutes

Mornay Sauce Preparation:

Melt butter in heavy medium saucepan over medium heat.
Add flour and whisk until mixture is smooth, about 1 minute.
Whisk in milk and salt.
Whisk until mixture thickens slightly, about 2 minutes.
Gradually whisk in cheeses.
Stir until mixture is smooth and begins to bubble, stirring constantly, about 5 minutes.
Cover and keep warm.

Egg Pastry Crowns Preparation:

Meanwhile, preheat oven to 400 degrees.
Place pastry shells on a cookie sheet and bake for 12 minutes, or until golden on top.
Whisk eggs and milk in large bowl to blend.
Place a large nonstick skillet over medium heat.
Add oil and butter to skillet.
When the butter foams, add the egg mixture.
Stir continuously with a rubber spatula until eggs are light and fluffy, about 2 minutes.
Season to taste with salt and pepper.
Remove tops and hollow out pastry shells.
Divide scrambled eggs among pastries.
Top each with 2 to 3 tablespoons of Mornay Sauce.
Sprinkle with chives and serve.

Storage and Leftovers: Mornay Sauce can be stored for up to 2 days. Cover tightly and refrigerate.
Reheat over low heat, stirring constantly.

$$ Music: *Dee Cartensen, "Regarding the Soul"*

COUNTRY BISCUITS AND GRAVY

Nothing is better than old-fashioned biscuits, hot or cold. Then when they're smothered in gravy—look out. Whether you're making this wonderful down-home breakfast for one or ten, it's quick and easy and I promise it will hit the spot.

Serves 4

8	ounces (bulk) pork sausage, crumbled, *Jimmy Dean*®
1	can (10.5-ounce) white sauce, *Aunt Penny's*®
3/4	cup whole milk
	Salt and pepper
1	container (10.2-ounce) prepared buttermilk biscuit dough, *Pillsbury Grands*®

Prep time: 5 minutes
Cooking time: 12 minutes

Preparation:

In a small skillet over medium heat, sauté sausage until thoroughly cooked, about 4 minutes.
Add white sauce and milk.
Bring to a simmer.
Cover and simmer 2 minutes to blend flavors.
Season to taste with salt and pepper.
Meanwhile, bake biscuits according to package instructions.
Cut baked biscuits in half and place 2 halves on each plate.
Spoon sausage gravy generously over tops of biscuits and serve.

Storage and Leftovers: Store biscuits in a resealable bag at room temperature for up to 2 days. Cover gravy tightly and store in refrigerator for up to 2 days. To reheat, combine gravy and reduced-fat milk (as needed) in a saucepan over low heat, stirring constantly until warm.

$$

Music: *Catie Curtis, "Truth from Lies"*

DATE-NUT CARROT MUFFINS

Makes 12 muffins

	Nonstick vegetable cooking spray, *PAM®*
1	package (16.6-ounce) date muffin mix, *Pillsbury®*
1	cup wheat bran
1	cup whole milk
1	egg
1	cup shredded carrots, *Mann's®*
3/4	cup pitted dates, chopped (dates may be available already chopped), *Sunsweet®*

Prep time: 5 minutes
Cooking time: 20 minutes

P r e p a r a t i o n :

Preheat oven to 400 degrees.
Line 12 muffin tins with muffin papers or spray with nonstick spray.
In a medium bowl, stir muffin mix, bran, milk, and egg until just blended.
Fold in carrots and dates (do not overmix; the batter should be lumpy).
Divide batter equally among muffin tins.
Bake until a toothpick inserted into center of muffin comes out clean, about 20 minutes.
Serve warm or at room temperature.

Storage and Leftovers: Store in an airtight container for up to 2 days.

$

Music: *Carrie Newcomer, "Visions and Dreams"*

EGGS IN A NEST

Chez? Cheez Whiz®! Cheez Whiz®? Everyone who's anyone in the food business has informed me that this book will receive the worst reviews if I include Cheez Whiz® in any of my recipes! But it tastes so good and consistently has a perfect texture. So my apologies to the food critics and purists—but this recipe is wonderful!

Serves 4

	Nonstick vegetable cooking spray, *PAM®*
6	eggs
1/2	teaspoon ground black pepper, *McCormick®*
1/2	teaspoon seasoned salt, *Lawry's®*
2	tablespoons butter, *Land O'Lakes®*
4	slices light whole wheat bread, *Wonder®*
8	teaspoons Cheez Whiz®, *Kraft®*

Prep time: 8 minutes
Cooking time: 8 minutes

Preparation:

Preheat oven to 325 degrees.
Spray four 1-cup ovenproof custard or dessert cups with nonstick spray.
In a large bowl, whisk eggs, pepper, and seasoned salt until foamy.
In a large nonstick skillet over medium heat, melt 1 tablespoon butter.
Add egg mixture and stir constantly for about 2 minutes, or until eggs are almost set.
Spread remaining 1 tablespoon butter over 1 side of each bread slice (this prevents
   eggs from making the bread soggy).
Place 1 bread slice, buttered side up, in each cup, pressing to fit.
Spoon 1 teaspoon of Cheez Whiz® on top of each bread slice.
Divide eggs equally among cups.
Spoon 1 teaspoon of Cheez Whiz® on top of each.
Bake until cheese is melted, about 5 minutes.
Serve hot.

Note: Garnish with shredded cheese and chopped tomatoes, if desired.

$ Music: *Tracy Chapman, "Telling Stories"*

CRISPY RICE PUDDING

Pudding for breakfast? Am I nuts? It might seem that way, but while we were photographing this breakfast, everyone in my kitchen ate bowls and bowls of this palate-pleasing rice pudding. Once you taste it you'll understand why! If you're still hesitant, at least try it for a snack. I don't want you to miss out.

Serves 2

2	containers (3.5 ounces each) refrigerated prepared vanilla pudding, *Jell-O®*
3/4	cup Rice Krispies® cereal, *Kellogg's®*
1/4	cup golden raisins, *Dole®*
1	teaspoon ground cinnamon, *McCormick®*

Prep time: 3 minutes

P r e p a r a t i o n :

Divide pudding between two 1-cup ramekins.
Mix cereal, raisins, and cinnamon in a medium bowl.
Spoon even portions of the raisin mixture over pudding and serve, or cover tightly and
   refrigerate up to 8 hours.

$ Music: *Enya, "A Day Without Rain"*

STRAWBERRY BANANA BREAD PUDDING

Serves 10

	Nonstick vegetable cooking spray, *PAM®*
1	container (16-ounce) frozen sweetened sliced strawberries (about 2 cups), thawed and drained (reserve syrup and set aside)
1	package (13.9-ounce) banana quick bread mix, *Betty Crocker®*
2	eggs
3	tablespoons canola oil, *Wesson®*
1	container (8-ounce) mixed berry yogurt, *Colombo®*
1	cup plain yogurt, *Colombo®*

Prep time: 5 minutes
Cooking time: 50 minutes
Cooling time: 15 minutes

Preparation:

Preheat oven to 375 degrees.
Spray bottom of an 8x4x3-inch loaf pan with nonstick spray.
Stir 1 1/4 cups strawberries, banana bread mix, eggs, and oil in a large bowl to blend.
Transfer batter to prepared pan.
Bake until a toothpick inserted into center of bread comes out clean, about 50 minutes.
Cool 15 minutes in pan.
Remove bread from pan.
Meanwhile, stir remaining 3/4 cup strawberries (with syrup), berry yogurt, and plain
   yogurt in medium bowl to blend.
Cover and refrigerate until ready to serve.
Cut bread crosswise into 10 slices.
Transfer slices to plates.
Top with dollop of yogurt mixture and serve.

$$

Music: *Tasmin Archer, "Great Expectations"*

LUNCH

Lighter, smaller portions eaten at noon can be as appetizing and satisfying as dinner. Lunches shared with coworkers, friends, or family are always a midday delight. Looking back on my childhood, one of the highlights of my day was the delectable surprise awaiting me at lunchtime. Little did I know how necessary lunch is toward maintaining a healthy attitude and high energy level. Now, lunch is about taking a little personal time to enjoy a meal, catch up, and catch my breath.

Often, lunch can seem uneventful and humdrum, especially when it's the same old selection in the fridge, or when there is nothing appealing at the local restaurants, delis, or fast-food chains. Semi-Homemade lunches will entice the pickiest of palates and put the pizzazz back into your noonday breaks. You will find recipes suitable for weekdays or weekends, intimate lunches or playtime pow-wows.

Whether you want to eat light, are feeling famished, or just want something healthful to nosh, there is much here to choose from. Best of all, each recipe is quick to make and tastes great whether eaten at home or the office.

Lunch

PEPPER PEACH CHICKEN SKEWER

It was hard to decide where to place this recipe. These pepper peach chicken skewers could easily have gone in appetizers (they're perfect for guests) or in dinners (just use longer skewers and more chicken and peaches). But lunches fill the bill since I eat these mostly on Saturday or Sunday afternoon. Feel free to serve them anytime, they'll always be welcome. By the way, I think you'll be happily surprised at how well pepper and peach complement each other.

Makes 24 pieces

24	wood skewers
1	tablespoon olive oil, *Bertolli®*
1	tablespoon lemon juice, or *ReaLemon®*
2	teaspoons minced fresh garlic, *McCormick®*
1	teaspoon pepper, *McCormick®*
3/4	teaspoon ground cumin, *McCormick®*
4	boneless skinless chicken breasts, each cut into 6 cubes
2	firm ripe peaches, pitted, each cut into 12 cubes
	Salt

Prep time: 30 minutes
Cooking time: 12 minutes

Preparation:

Soak wood skewers in water for 10 minutes.
In a medium bowl, mix oil, lemon juice, garlic, pepper, and cumin for marinade.
Toss chicken cubes in the marinade.
Cover and refrigerate for 20 minutes.
Preheat broiler.
Place 1 chicken cube and 1 peach cube onto each skewer.
Sprinkle with salt.
Place on a broiler pan.
Broil until chicken is cooked through and beginning to brown. Turn skewers halfway
   through cooking to brown on all sides, about 12 minutes total.
Arrange skewers on platter and serve immediately.

$$ Music: *Afro Celt Sound System, Volume 2: Release, "Fire Under: World Dance"*

BLACK BEAN QUESADILLA

Mexican food is my favorite food of all. My husband, Bruce, would tell you that I could eat Mexican food morning, noon, and night. It's true. This recipe is quick and delicious and is one of my favorites. It's easy and so fast to make.

Serves 2

2	burrito-size flour tortillas, *Mission®*
1	cup canned refried low-fat black beans, *Rosarito®*
1	cup chunky salsa, *Pace®*
1	cup Mexican-style shredded cheese, *Kraft®*
1/2	cup prepared guacamole (refrigerated section)
2	tablespoons sour cream

Prep time: 5 minutes
Cooking time: 15 minutes

Preparation:

Preheat oven to 400 degrees.
Lay 1 tortilla on a clean work surface.
Spread the beans evenly over the tortilla.
Spoon 3/4 cup of the salsa over the beans, then sprinkle with the cheese.
Top with the second tortilla.
Place the quesadilla on a foil-covered cookie sheet.
Bake for approximately 15 minutes, or until the cheese is melted and the top is crisp
    and brown.
Meanwhile, swirl the guacamole and sour cream together in a small bowl.
Cut the quesadilla into 4 equal portions and transfer to a plate.
Serve with the guacamole mixture and remaining 1/4 cup of salsa.

Storage and Leftovers: Cover tightly and refrigerate; store for up to one day. Reheat in a 400-degree
    oven for about 10 minutes or until hot.

$$ Music: *Sting, "Brand New Day"*

SOUTHWESTERN TURKEY CHILI AND CORN BREAD

Canned chili got me through my college years. I put it in omelets, poured it over biscuits, and sometimes would eat it right out of the can. It was hearty, satisfying, and affordable. At the time I didn't even think about what the meat content might be—thank goodness, because I would have starved. But here's a way to tantalize your taste buds with an all-time favorite by using vegetarian-like products and your own fresh meat. This chili is fantastic for football Sundays. Let me know what your friends and family think about this recipe! (See page 204.)

Serves 2

CORN BREAD:

	Nonstick vegetable cooking spray, *PAM®*
1	can (11-ounce) Mexicorn, *Green Giant®*
1	egg
1	package (8 1/2-ounce) corn muffin mix, *Jiffy®*

CHILI:

10	ounces lean ground turkey, crumbled
1	tablespoon all-purpose flour, *Pillsbury®*
1	tablespoon olive oil, *Bertolli®*
1	can (15.5-ounce) spicy black beans, *S&W Regional Recipe: San Antonio Beans®*
1	can (14 1/2-ounce) stewed tomatoes, Mexican recipe style, *S&W®*
	Garnishes: sour cream, chopped fresh cilantro, chopped red onion

Prep time:	5 minutes
Cooking time:	25 minutes

Corn Bread Preparation:

Preheat oven to 400 degrees.
Spray 8x8x2-inch baking pan with nonstick spray.
Drain all but 2 tablespoons liquid from Mexicorn.
Place reserved 2 tablespoons liquid in a medium bowl.
Add egg to liquid and whisk to blend.
Stir in Mexicorn.
Add corn muffin mix and stir until just blended.
Transfer mixture to prepared pan.
Bake until a toothpick inserted into center of corn bread comes out clean, about 20 minutes.

Chili Preparation:

Meanwhile, in a Ziploc® bag, toss turkey with flour, until flour is absorbed into meat.
Heat oil in a wide 2-quart pot over medium heat.
Sauté the turkey until browned, about 5 minutes.
Add the beans and tomatoes.
Simmer over medium low heat until chili is slightly thick, about 8 minutes.
Spoon chili into bowls.
Top with sour cream, cilantro, and onion.
Serve hot with corn bread.

Storage and Leftovers: Cover tightly and store corn bread at room temperature for up to 3 days. Cover tightly and store chili in refrigerator for up to 3 days. Reheat over medium heat.

$$

Music: *Spinners, "The Best of the Spinners"*

GNOCCHI DIPPERS

Serves 4

1	package (9-ounce) gnocchi (dry pasta section), *Alessi®* or substitute with cheese tortellini pasta, *Rosetto®*
2	teaspoons olive oil, *Bertolli®*
1/4	onion, minced
2	teaspoons minced fresh garlic, *McCormick®*
1	package (8-ounce) Velveeta® cheese, *Kraft®*
1/2	cup reduced-fat milk
1/4	teaspoon hot sauce, *Tabasco®*
8	teaspoons light sour cream
	fresh thyme sprigs (optional)

Prep time: 4 minutes
Cooking time: 10 minutes

Preparation:

Prepare gnocchi according to package instructions.
Heat oil in a medium saucepan over medium heat.
Sauté onion and garlic in oil until onion is tender, about 2 minutes.
Add the cheese, milk, and hot sauce.
Stir until sauce is smooth and cheese has completely melted, about 4 minutes.
Fold cooked gnocchi into sauce.
Transfer gnocchi and sauce to 4 bowls.
Top each serving with 2 teaspoons sour cream and serve immediately.
Garnish with thyme (optional).

Storage and Leftovers: Cover tightly and store in refrigerator for up to 2 days. To reheat, combine gnocchi and reduced-fat milk (as needed) in a saucepan over medium heat, stirring frequently until warm.

$$ \hspace{6cm} Music: *Les Nubians, "Princesses Nubiennes"*

PROSCIUTTO AND GOAT CHEESE PIZZA

I love this pizza; love this pizza; am in love with this pizza! It's delicious, and once you put the first bite in your mouth, you'll be in love with it too! It's simple, quick, and fun to make.

Serves 2

1	fully baked thin pizza crust (10-ounce), *Boboli®*
1/2	cup marinara sauce, *Boboli®*
1	cup shredded mozzarella cheese, *Kraft®*
1	package (3-ounce) thinly sliced prosciutto (deli section), *Citterio®*
1	ounce soft fresh goat cheese, coarsely crumbled
2	tablespoons fresh basil, chopped

Prep time: 6 minutes
Cooking time: 12 minutes

Preparation:

Preheat oven to 425 degrees.
Lay pizza crust on a foil-covered pizza pan or cookie sheet.
Spread sauce evenly over pizza crust.
Sprinkle mozzarella cheese over crust, leaving a 1-inch border around edge.
Arrange prosciutto on top of cheese.
Sprinkle goat cheese over prosciutto.
Bake until prosciutto is crisp and cheeses are melted, about 12 minutes.
Sprinkle basil over pizza.
Cut pizza into 6 slices and serve.

Storage and Leftovers: Cover tightly and store in refrigerator for up to 2 days. Reheat in a 425-degree oven for about 10 minutes or until warm.

$$

Music: *Martin Sexton, "The American"*

CURRIED BOWTIE SALAD

Serves 4

3/4	cup sour cream
2	teaspoons curry powder, *McCormick®*
2	cans (8 ounces each) pineapple chunks, drained, *Dole®*
1	ripe medium avocado, peeled, pitted, and sliced
1	medium red apple, cored and sliced
16	ounces bowtie-shaped pasta/farfalle (prepare 8 ounces, half of package), *De Cecco®*
	Salt

Prep time: 10 minutes
Cooking time: 5 minutes
Cooling time: 15 minutes

Preparation:

In a large bowl, mix sour cream and curry powder to blend.
Fold in pineapple, avocado, and apple.
Meanwhile, cook pasta in a pot of boiling salted water until just tender, about 5
    minutes. Drain.
Rinse pasta under cold water to cool, then let drain well.
Fold pasta into sour cream mixture.
Refrigerate until cold, about 15 minutes.
Season salad to taste with salt and serve.

Note: Salad can be served on a bed of shredded red cabbage or on fresh baby spinach.
Storage and Leftovers: Cover tightly and store in refrigerator for up to 1 day.

$$

Music: *Doobie Brothers, "Best of the Doobies"*

BEEFY STEW

When making stew I've always liked using a canned vegetable soup and then adding my own choice of fresh meat to it. It tastes much better than ordinary canned stew and it's fresher. This stew recipe makes a wonderfully hearty meal. Double or triple the recipe and keep it in the fridge—it makes great leftovers, too!

Serves 4

1	sheet frozen puff pastry, thawed, cut into four 4-inch rounds, *Pepperidge Farm®*
1 1/2	pounds beef cube steak, cut into 1-inch pieces
	Salt and pepper
2	tablespoons all-purpose flour, *Pillsbury®*
1/4	cup vegetable oil, *Wesson®*
1	can (14-ounce) reduced-sodium beef broth, *Swanson®*
1	jar (24-ounce) country vegetable soup, *Campbell's®*

Prep time: 10 minutes
Cooking time: 35 minutes

Preparation:

Position rack in center of oven and preheat to 425 degrees.
Arrange puff pastry rounds on a large heavy cookie sheet.
Bake pastry rounds until puffed, golden brown, and cooked through, about 12 minutes.
Set aside and keep warm.
Meanwhile, sprinkle beef with salt and pepper.
Toss beef with flour in a large bowl to coat.
Heat oil in a heavy large casserole over medium high heat.
Add one-third of the beef to oil and sauté until brown, about 5 minutes.
Using a slotted spoon, transfer beef to bowl.
Repeat with remaining beef.
Add beef broth and bring to a simmer, stirring to loosen browned bits on bottom.
Return all beef and any accumulated juices to casserole.
Add soup and simmer uncovered, until liquid thickens slightly and beef is tender, about 15 minutes.
Divide stew equally among 4 bowls.
Top each with a warm puff pastry round and serve.

Storage and Leftovers: Store puff pastries in a resealable bag at room temperature for up to 2 days. Cover tightly and store Beefy Stew in refrigerator for up to 2 days. To reheat, combine Beefy Stew and 1/4 cup water in a saucepan over medium heat, stirring frequently until warm.

$$

Music: *Faire Celts, Various Artists, "A Woman's Voice"*

SALAD CHINOIS

This salad is a sleeper! It's never the first thing anyone ever makes, but I guarantee once you try it you'll be hooked. Here's a little secret: I make the dressing and serve it as a dip—it's the best—you'll want to put it on everything.

Serves 4

DRESSING:

2/3	cup mayonnaise, *Best Foods®* or *Hellmann's®*
2	tablespoons reduced-sodium soy sauce, *Kikkoman®*
1	teaspoon ground ginger, *McCormick®*

SALAD:

1	can (10-ounce) premium chunk chicken breast, drained and chilled, *Swanson®*
2	cups coleslaw mix (shredded cabbage and carrots, without sauce), *Ready Pac®*
1	can (14-ounce) chow mein vegetables, drained and chilled, *Chun King®*
1	bag (5-ounce) prepared green salad, *Fresh Express®*
1	can (5-ounce) chow mein noodles, *La Choy®*
1	can (11-ounce) mandarin orange segments, drained and chilled, *Dole®*

Prep time: 10 minutes

Dressing Preparation:

In a small bowl, mix mayonnaise, soy sauce, and ginger to blend.

Salad Preparation:

In a large bowl, toss chicken, coleslaw mix, and drained chow mein vegetables until well mixed.
Toss chicken mixture with enough dressing to coat well.
Line individual bowls or plates with a small amount of green salad.
Spoon chicken mixture on top of green salad.
Garnish with noodles and orange segments before serving.

Note: Serve with fresh melon skewers or sliced fresh pineapple.
Storage and Leftovers: Cover tightly and store in refrigerator for up to 1 day.

$$

Music: *Madonna, "Ray of Light"*

SIX-CHEESE TORTELLINI

Serves 4

2	tablespoons butter, *Land O'Lakes®*
I	cup whole milk
1/4	cup Cheez Whiz®, *Kraft®*
I	package (8-ounce) shredded Six-Cheese Italian Blend (mozzarella, smoked provolone, Parmesan, Romano, Fontina, and Asiago cheeses), *Sargento®*
1/8	teaspoon cayenne pepper, *McCormick®*
2	packages (9 ounces each) fresh cheese tortellini (refrigerated section), *Rosetto®*

Prep time: 5 minutes
Cooking time: 12 minutes

Preparation:

Melt butter in a heavy large saucepan over medium heat.
Add milk and bring to a simmer.
Whisk in Cheez Whiz®.
Gradually whisk in shredded cheeses.
Stir until cheeses melt and mixture begins to bubble, about 5 minutes.
Whisk in cayenne.
Meanwhile, cook tortellini in a pot of boiling salted water until just tender, about 4
  minutes. Drain.
Add tortellini to cheese sauce.
Toss to coat.
Divide tortellini and sauce equally among 6 pasta bowls and serve.

*Note: Can be made 1 day ahead. Transfer tortellini and sauce to a 2-quart baking dish. Cover
  and bake until heated through, about 25 minutes.*
*Storage and Leftovers: Cover tightly and store in refrigerator for up to 2 days. To reheat, combine
  tortellini and whole milk (as needed) in a saucepan over medium heat, stirring frequently
  until warm.*

$$ Music: *Everything but the Girl, "Walking Wounded"*

DINNER

Dinner should be seen as a celebration that ends another productive day. It's a time to reflect and share ideas, new happenings, and current events. It's also a time for you and yours to relax and unwind, a time for families to bond and communicate while reinforcing the security and stability of home. Dinner should be a pleasure—a time to laugh, have fun, and enjoy one another's company. It shouldn't be yet another stressful "to-do" on your list. Preparing dinner can be easy and satisfying with Semi-Homemade recipes.

Many of us have dinner on the run. For you domestic goddesses, bad habits are easily formed as you constantly try to squeeze your families' dinner in between soccer practice, homework, and last-minute errands. For you corporate devotees, take-out and eating at your desk is commonplace when trying to meet demanding deadlines. Regardless, both scenarios are unhealthful and rob everyone of the important downtime and pleasure of a good meal. Semi-Homemade dinners are simple to make and give you more time to enjoy yourself and others without sacrificing taste or nutrition. Bon appétit!

DIJON CHICKEN AND MUSHROOMS

Anyone who's ever eaten with me would describe me as one of the pickiest eaters they've ever seen, and chicken has never been my favorite. However, several years ago I had one of the most amazing meals ever, Dijon Chicken and Mushrooms. It took me nearly two years to perfect this recipe and two minutes to clean my plate.

Serves 4

4	boneless skinless chicken breasts (about 6 ounces each)
	Salt and pepper
2	tablespoons butter, *Land O'Lakes®*
8	white button mushrooms, finely chopped
I	can (10-ounce) condensed fat-free cream of mushroom soup, *Campbell's®*
1/2	cup canned chicken broth, *Swanson®*
1/4	cup Dijon mustard, *French's®*
2	tablespoons deli-style brown mustard, *French's®*
I	tomato, diced
1/4	cup frozen corn kernels, thawed
1/4	cup chopped fresh chives

Prep time: 7 minutes
Cooking time: 25 minutes

Preparation:

Sprinkle chicken with salt and pepper.
Melt butter in a heavy large skillet over medium high heat.
Add chicken and cook until just brown, about 4 minutes per side.
Transfer chicken to plate.
Add mushrooms to the same skillet and sauté until tender, about 3 minutes.
Whisk in soup, broth, and mustards.
Bring sauce to a simmer.
Return chicken to skillet and submerge into sauce completely.
Reduce heat to medium low.
Cover and cook until soup bubbles thickly and chicken is cooked through, about
    10 minutes.
Transfer chicken to plates and spoon sauce over the top.
Sprinkle with tomatoes, corn, and chives.
Serve hot.

$$

Wine: *De Loach® Chardonnay*
Music: *Etta James, "At Last"*

STEAK PINWHEELS WITH SUN-DRIED TOMATO STUFFING AND ROSEMARY MASHED POTATOES

Serves 4 to 6

STEAK:

1 2/3	cups canned beef broth, *Swanson®*
3/4	cup ready-to-use julienne sun-dried tomatoes (not packed in oil), *Frieda's®*
1/4	cup butter, *Land O'Lakes®*
1	package (6.6-ounce) stuffing mix, *Stove Top®* (flavor optional)
1	1 1/4-pound skirt steak
	Salt and pepper

ROSEMARY MASHED POTATOES:

2	packages (11 ounces each) refrigerated prepared mashed potatoes, *Simply Potatoes®*
6	tablespoons butter, *Land O'Lakes®*
1/4	cup whole milk
2	teaspoons fresh rosemary, finely chopped
	Salt and pepper

Prep time:	12 minutes
Cooking time:	50 minutes

Steak Preparation:

Bring broth, sun-dried tomatoes, and butter to a boil in a medium saucepan. Stir in contents of stuffing mix pouch. Cover saucepan and remove from heat. Let stand 5 minutes. Fluff stuffing with fork. Cool stuffing. Preheat oven to 425 degrees. Lay steak flat on clean work surface. Sprinkle steak with salt and pepper. Cover steak evenly with stuffing. Roll up steak lengthwise to create a pinwheel effect, enclosing stuffing completely. Skewer seam with toothpicks. Place the steak roll, seam side down, on a foil-covered cookie sheet. Sprinkle roll with salt and pepper. Roast until steak is golden brown and cooked through, about 40 minutes.

Rosemary Mashed Potatoes Preparation:

Meanwhile, peel back corners of potato packages. Warm potatoes in microwave according to package instructions. Mix in butter, milk, and rosemary. Season potatoes to taste with salt and pepper.

Note: May be served with my More-Than-Meatloaf Gravy (recipe found in Gravies and Sauces chapter).

$$$

Wine: *Kendall-Jackson® Cabernet Sauvignon*
Music: *Hi Fidelity Lounge, Various Artists, "Volume I: Subterranean Soundtracks"*

MEATY MICROWAVE LASAGNA

Serves 6 to 8

1 1/2	pounds ground beef
3	jars (14 ounces each) tomato and basil pasta sauce, *Classico®*
1	package (1.5-ounce) spaghetti sauce mix, *McCormick®*
2	teaspoons minced fresh garlic, *McCormick®*
1	package (16-ounce) lasagna noodles, *De Cecco®*
1	container (16-ounce) small curd cottage cheese
3	packages (6 ounces each) sliced mozzarella cheese, *Sargento®*
1	cup shredded Parmesan cheese, *Kraft®*

Prep time:	10 minutes
Cooking time:	30 minutes
Cooling time:	15 minutes

Preparation:

Sauté ground beef in a heavy large skillet over medium high heat until brown, about 5 minutes.

Mix in pasta sauce, spaghetti sauce mix, and garlic.

Simmer 2 minutes to blend flavors.

Layer 1 1/4 cups meat sauce, lasagna noodles, 2/3 cup cottage cheese, six slices mozzarella, and 1/4 cup Parmesan cheese (in that order) in a 13x9x2-inch microwave-safe baking dish.

Repeat layering 2 to 3 more times.

Top with remaining meat sauce.

Cover baking dish tightly with plastic wrap.

Microwave on high for 15 minutes.

Carefully remove plastic wrap.

Arrange remaining 6 slices mozzarella over lasagna.

Sprinkle remaining 1/4 cup Parmesan over lasagna.

Cover with plastic wrap and cook until noodles are tender and cheese melts, about 5 minutes.

Uncover and let cool 10-15 minutes before serving.

Note: Serve with garlic bread and a mixed green salad.
Storage and Leftovers: Cover tightly and store lasagna in refrigerator for up to 3 days. To reheat, slice lasagna into individual servings, cover each serving loosely, and microwave for about 2 1/2 minutes, or until warm in center.

$$$

Wine: *Gallo of Sonoma® Merlot*
Music: *Francis Albert Sinatra & Antonio Carlos Jobim*

LEMON TURKEY CUTLETS

Serves 4

1 1/2	pounds refrigerated boneless turkey cutlets, *The Turkey Store®*
	Salt and pepper
1/3	cup all-purpose flour, *Pillsbury®*
1	egg, beaten to blend
2	tablespoons fresh lemon juice, or *ReaLemon®*
1	cup Italian style bread crumbs, *Progresso®*
2	tablespoons finely chopped onion
1/3	cup vegetable oil, *Wesson®*

Prep time:	8 minutes
Cooking time:	12 minutes

Preparation:

Rinse cutlets with cold water and pat dry with paper towels.

Sprinkle cutlets with salt and pepper.

Place flour in a medium bowl.

In another medium bowl, combine egg and lemon juice.

In a third medium bowl, combine bread crumbs and onion.

Heat oil in a large skillet over medium high heat.

Working in batches, dip cutlets into flour, then egg, and then bread crumbs.

Place cutlets in hot oil and cook until brown, about 3 minutes per side.

Note: May be served with my Creamy Mustard Sauce (recipe found in Gravies and Sauces chapter).

$$$

Wine: *Chateau St. Michelle® Chardonnay*
Music: *Various Artists, "Soul Food"*

RAVIOLI STROGANOFF

My husband loves pasta as much as I love Mexican food. So I've learned some simple, sumptuous ways to be creative. This mushroom cream sauce is extraordinary and the ground turkey adds a new tasty twist. I've learned to love pasta almost as much as my husband does. Maybe my next book should be 50 percent Mexican food, 50 percent Italian food. Should I call it "Tortillas to Pasta" or "Pasta to Tortillas"? Let me know your thoughts (see page 204).

Serves 4

1	package (25-ounce) refrigerated cheese ravioli, *Rosetto®*
2	teaspoons vegetable oil, *Wesson®*
1	pound lean ground turkey
1/2	teaspoon Italian Seasoning: Classic Herbs, *McCormick®*
1	can (10 3/4-ounce) condensed cream of mushroom soup, *Campbell's®*
1	cup whole milk
3/4	cup sour cream

Prep time: 10 minutes
Cooking time: 15 minutes

Preparation:

Prepare ravioli according to package instructions; drain and set aside.
Meanwhile, in a medium frying pan, heat oil over high heat.
Add turkey and seasoning,
Sauté until turkey is brown, breaking it into 1-inch pieces with a spatula, about 6 minutes.
Stir in soup and milk.
Bring to a simmer.
Remove from heat.
Stir in sour cream.
Gently toss ravioli in sauce to coat.
Transfer to plates and serve.

$$

Wine: *1999 Lindeman Bin® Pinot Nior*
Music: *Maxwell, "Embrya"*

SWEET AND SOUR PORK KABOBS WITH FRIED RICE

Serves 4

KABOBS:

1/3	cup sweet and sour sauce, *Dynasty®*
1/4	cup pineapple juice from canned pineapple, *Dole®*
2	tablespoons soy sauce, *Kikkoman®*
1	garlic clove, minced
1	teaspoon fresh ginger, peeled and minced
1	pound pork tenderloin, cut crosswise into 12 equal pieces
4	button mushrooms
4	cherry tomatoes
1	small zucchini, cut crosswise into 4 equal pieces
1/2	green bell pepper, quartered
1/2	red bell pepper, quartered
1/2	can (8-ounce) pineapple chunks, drained, *Dole®*
4	10-inch wood skewers, soaked in water 10 minutes to keep from burning

FRIED RICE:

1	package (6.25-ounce) fried rice, *Rice-A-Roni®*
1	tablespoon butter, *Land O'Lakes®*
1 1/2	cups water
2	tablespoons soy sauce, *Kikkoman®*
1/3	cup frozen peas and carrots, thawed, *Green Giant®*
1/4	cup frozen cut corn kernels, thawed, *Green Giant®*

Prep time:	30 minutes
Cooking time:	20 minutes

Kabobs Preparation:

In a small bowl, mix first 5 ingredients together. Set marinade aside. Place pork in a medium bowl. In another medium bowl, place vegetables and pineapple. Distribute marinade evenly between the 2 bowls and toss pork to coat. Refrigerate at least 15 minutes, or up to 8 hours. Preheat broiler. Alternate pork, vegetables, and pineapple evenly on 4 skewers. Place skewers on a broiler pan and broil until pork is cooked through and beginning to brown, turning skewers halfway through cooking, about 5 minutes per side.

Fried Rice Preparation:

Meanwhile, combine rice-vermicelli mix from fried rice package (reserve seasonings) and butter in a heavy large skillet. Sauté over medium heat until vermicelli is golden brown, about 2 minutes. Gradually add 1 1/2 cups water, soy sauce, and special seasonings from fried rice package. Bring to a boil. Cover skillet. Reduce heat to low. Simmer until rice is tender, about 15 minutes. Remove skillet from heat. Sprinkle peas, carrots, and corn over rice mixture. Cover and let rice stand 5 minutes. Using fork, fluff rice and mix in peas, carrots, and corn.

$$

Wine: *Hugel® Gentil*
Music: *Celine Dion, "The French Album"*

MUSHROOM STEAK AND SWEET MASH

Serves 4

MUSHROOM STEAK:
4	beef cube steaks (about 4 ounces each)
	Salt and pepper
1/2	cup all-purpose flour, *Pillsbury*®
1/4	cup vegetable oil, *Wesson*®
2	cans (14 ounces each) beef broth, *Swanson*®
1	can (10-ounce) condensed golden mushroom soup, *Campbell's*®
1	white onion, cut into 1/4-inch-thick slices and separated into rings

SWEET MASH:
1	can (15-ounce) cut sweet potatoes, drained and rinsed, *Princella*®
1/2	cup whole milk
4	tablespoons butter, *Land O'Lakes*®
2	tablespoons golden brown sugar, *C&H*®
	Salt and pepper
1	package (11-ounce) refrigerated prepared mashed potatoes, *Simply Potatoes*®

Prep time:	5 minutes
Cooking time:	40 minutes

Mushroom Steak Preparation:

Sprinkle steaks generously with salt and pepper. Place flour in large soup plate or pie pan. Dredge steaks in flour, coating completely. Heat oil in a large skillet on medium high heat. Fry two floured steaks in skillet until just brown, about 3 minutes per side. Transfer steaks to paper towel (to drain excess oil). Repeat with remaining steaks. Sprinkle remaining flour from plate into remaining oil in skillet (do not remove pan drippings from skillet). Stir continuously until paste is dark brown, about 3 minutes. Reduce heat to low. Whisk in beef broth. Stir in soup. Return steaks to skillet, submerging in gravy completely. Top with onion rings. Cover and simmer for 20 minutes, or until gravy is thick. Season gravy to taste with salt and pepper.

Sweet Mash Preparation:

Meanwhile, using a fork, mash sweet potatoes in a medium microwave-safe bowl. Mix in 1/4 cup milk, 2 tablespoons butter, and brown sugar. Cover tightly with plastic wrap and cook in microwave on high until hot, about 3 minutes. Season sweet potatoes to taste with salt and pepper. Set aside and keep warm. Peel back corner of mashed potatoes package. Warm potatoes in microwave according to package instructions. Mix in remaining 1/4 cup milk and 2 tablespoons butter. Season potatoes to taste with salt and pepper.

Presentation:

On each plate, swirl mashed potatoes with sweet potatoes. Place steak on top of potatoes. Smother steaks with gravy. Garnish with onions and serve.

$$$

Wine: *Beringer North Coast*® *Zinfandel*
Music: *Sting, "Nada Como El Sol"*

TROPICAL SALMON

When I moved to Los Angeles from Wisconsin, I rented a room in a house from two German men and a Portuguese woman—there is no punch line here. One of the men was a private chef for the rich and famous and shared many of his secret recipes with me. This was one of his favorites, and now I am so happy to be sharing it with you. It's perfect for a romantic evening and will make you look brilliant.

Serves 2

TROPICAL RICE:

1	bag white rice, *Uncle Ben's Boil-In-Bag Rice®*
1/4	cup dried tropical fruit mix, *Sunsweet® Fruitlings®*
1/4	cup dry roasted peanuts, chopped, *Planters®*

SALMON AND CHIVE SAUCE:

2	tablespoons tartar sauce, *Kraft®*
2	tablespoons sour cream
2	tablespoons fresh lime juice
1	tablespoon Dijon mustard, *French's®*
2	teaspoons fresh chives, chopped
1	skinless salmon fillet (12-ounce), cut crosswise into ten 1/2-inch-thick slices Fresh dill (optional)

Prep time:	15 minutes
Cooking time:	20 minutes

Tropical Rice Preparation:

Prepare rice according to package instructions, adding dried fruit halfway through the cooking time.
Remove rice from heat.
Mix in nuts.
Transfer rice to serving bowl.

Salmon and Chive Sauce Preparation:

Meanwhile, in a small bowl, mix tartar sauce, sour cream, lime juice, mustard, and chives.
Cover chive sauce and refrigerate.
Preheat broiler.
Divide salmon slices between two broilerproof glass or ceramic plates, covering half of each of the plates.
Place plates under broiler and cook until salmon is pale pink and flaky, watching salmon carefully so it does not overcook, about 1 minute.
Using potholders, carefully remove hot plates.
Spoon chive sauce on top of salmon and serve with rice.
Garnish with fresh dill (optional).

$$$

Wine: *Meridian® Chardonnay*
Music: *Barry White, "The Icon is Love"*

SPEEDY SWEDISH MEATBALLS

I've been to some of the most acclaimed restaurants in the world—and loved every minute. But I must admit I truly love a good old-fashioned smorgasbord. Some of my friends are cringing right now—but I find smorgasbord food to be quite good, fun, and a great value. I always go directly for the Swedish meatballs. So when creating this book, it was on the top of my list to include my very own Swedish meatball dinner—giving it a bit more of an upscale twist by adding broad egg noodles.

Serves 4

1/4	cup vegetable oil, *Wesson*®
2	pounds frozen beef meatballs (32-ounce), thawed, *Oh Boy*®
2	tablespoons all-purpose flour, *Pillsbury*®
1	can (14-ounce) reduced-sodium beef broth, *Swanson*®
1 1/2	cups whole milk
1/4	cup sour cream
1	package (8.8-ounce) egg noodles, *De Cecco*®

Prep time: 5 minutes
Cooking time: 15 minutes

Preparation:

Heat oil in a heavy large skillet over medium high heat.
Add meatballs and cook until brown, about 8 minutes.
Using tongs, transfer meatballs to a bowl.
Add flour to skillet and cook 1 minute, scraping up browned bits from bottom of skillet.
Stir in broth and milk.
Return meatballs to skillet.
Simmer until liquid thickens enough to coat meatballs, about 5 minutes.
Remove skillet from heat.
Stir in sour cream.
Meanwhile, cook noodles in a pot of boiling salted water until tender but still firm.
Drain.
Transfer noodles to a large bowl.
Spoon meatballs and sauce over noodles.
Serve immediately.

Storage and Leftovers: Cover tightly and store in refrigerator for up to 2 days. To reheat, combine meatballs and whole milk (as needed) in a saucepan over medium heat, stirring frequently, about 10 minutes or until warm. Cook fresh noodles when reserving.

$$

Wine: *Sonoma Creek*® *Merlot*
Music: *Simply Red, "Greatest Hits"*

NOODLES ALFREDO

For a little change of pace, I'm going to interview my husband, Bruce, on why he fancies this dish.

SL: Honey, why do you like this Noodles Alfredo dish so much?

Bruce: Because you're cooking it.

SL: Yes, honey, but I need a real answer.

Bruce: It's easy for you to make; it's great with a nice little salad and a bottle of wine; and it gives you a taste of Rome. Oh yeah—and it leaves you more time for me.

Serves 2

1	package (16-ounce) fettuccine (prepare 8 ounces, half of package), *De Cecco®*
1 1/2	sticks butter, *Land O'Lakes®*
1	cup whole milk
1	cup grated Parmesan cheese, *Kraft®*
	Salt

Prep time: 5 minutes
Cooking time: 10 minutes

Preparation:

In a large pot of boiling salted water, cook noodles according to package instructions.
Drain.
Return noodles to pot and place over low heat.
Add butter and milk to noodles and toss until butter is melted.
Add cheese and stir just until melted.
Remove from heat.
Salt to taste.
Serve immediately.

$

Wine: *Columbia Crest® Cabernet Sauvignon*
Music: *The London Symphony Orchestra, "Season for Love"*

DESSERTS

Like most people, I love desserts—they're my weakness. Growing up, I would sit in the kitchen for hours and watch my grandmother bake and decorate the most fabulous cakes. Unfortunately, none of us has time for this luxurious expression of love anymore. To this day, I have not forgotten my grandmother's greatest creations—her famous dessert casseroles. None of us ever knew exactly what was in them, but our mouths watered in anticipation of every bite. Now I, too, have continued her not-so-common tradition. Even my grandmother would take her hat off to the wonderful desserts included here. My decadent treats are not as time-consuming as the old-fashioned delicacies, but I promise you they are just as amazing and only you will know how truly easy they are to make.

BANANA PURSE

Makes 12

	Nonstick vegetable cooking spray, *PAM®*
3	bananas, peeled and thinly sliced
1/4	cup maple flavored pancake syrup, *Log Cabin Original Syrup®*
1	package frozen puff pastry (2 sheets), thawed, *Pepperidge Farm®*
1	tablespoon granulated sugar, *C&H®*
1	teaspoon ground cinnamon, *McCormick®*
2	tablespoons whole milk

Prep time: 10 minutes
Cooking time: 15 minutes

Preparation:

Position rack in center of oven and preheat to 400 degrees.
Line a heavy large cookie sheet with foil.
Spray foil with nonstick spray.
In a medium bowl, combine bananas and syrup.
Mash bananas slightly with a fork.
On a clean surface, lay flat 1 sheet of puff pastry.
Cut pastry in half lengthwise.
Using a rolling pin, roll out each pastry sheet into a 15x5-inch rectangle.
Cut each rectangle crosswise into thirds, forming 6 squares total.
Evenly distribute half of the banana mixture onto center of each square.
Fold corners of pastry into center and pinch ends together, twisting to seal.
Repeat with remaining sheet of puff pastry and banana mixture.
Arrange pastries on prepared cookie sheet.
In a small bowl, combine sugar and cinnamon.
Brush pastries with milk.
Sprinkle cinnamon-sugar over pastries.
Bake for 15 minutes, or until golden.
Serve warm.

$$

RASPBERRY TRIFLE WITH RUM SAUCE

Visually glorious and equally matched in flavor, this trifle is outrageously delicious and undoubtedly one of the most beautiful photographs we shot for this book. The entire crew admitted their mouths were watering, and so will yours once you taste it. Sinful!

Serves 6

3	tablespoons butter, *Land O'Lakes®*
3/4	cup confectioners/powdered sugar, *C&H®*
3/4	teaspoon imitation rum extract, *McCormick®*
3	tablespoons water
1/2	cup raspberry jam, *Knott's Berry Farm®*
1	frozen pound cake (12-ounce), thawed and cut into quarter-size cubes, *Sara Lee®*
3	containers (4 ounces each) refrigerated prepared vanilla pudding, *Jell-O®*
	Fresh raspberries

Prep time:	10 minutes
Cooking time:	1 minute
Set-up time:	45 minutes

Preparation:

Heat butter in a large glass bowl in microwave on high until melted, about 30 seconds.
Whisk in confectioners/powdered sugar, rum extract, and water, stirring to form a
    smooth sauce.
Heat jam in a small glass bowl in microwave on high until just melted, about 30 seconds.
In six small bowls or wineglasses, evenly distribute pound cake cubes.
Pack cubes down slightly.
Drizzle rum sauce and jam evenly over each.
Spoon 3 tablespoons of pudding evenly over each.
Refrigerate for 45 minutes.
Garnish with raspberries and serve.

$$

MALIBU® RUM CAKE

I created this cake in college and it was always a big hit. I wonder if having the word "rum" in its title added to its success?

Makes 1 large bundt cake, about 12 servings

CAKE:

	Nonstick vegetable cooking spray, *PAM®*
1	package (18.25-ounce) classic yellow cake mix, *Duncan Hines Moist Deluxe®*
1	cup *Malibu® Rum*
1/2	cup vegetable oil, *Wesson®*
1	package (3.4-ounce) vanilla instant pudding and pie filling mix, *Jell-O®*
4	eggs

RUM GLAZE:

1	cup (packed) golden brown sugar, *C&H®*
1/4	cup water
1	stick butter, *Land O'Lakes®*
1/4	cup *Malibu® Rum*

Prep time:	8 minutes
Cooking time:	45 minutes
Cooling time:	45 minutes

Cake Preparation:

Position rack in center of oven and preheat to 325 degrees.
Spray a 10-inch (12-cup) bundt pan with nonstick spray.
Using an electric mixer, beat all ingredients in a large bowl for 2 minutes.
Transfer batter to prepared pan.
Bake until a toothpick inserted in center of cake comes out clean, about 45 minutes.
Cool cake in pan for 20 minutes.
Invert cake onto platter, then carefully remove pan.
Allow cake to cool completely.

Rum Glaze Preparation:

Meanwhile, stir sugar and water in a heavy medium saucepan over medium high heat until sugar dissolves.
Add butter.
Simmer until mixture thickens and is syrupy, stirring often, about 5 minutes.
Remove saucepan from heat and whisk in rum.
Cool glaze completely.
Drizzle glaze evenly over cooled cake and serve.

Storage and Leftovers: Cover tightly and store rum cake at room temperature for up to 3 days. Cover tightly and store rum glaze in refrigerator for up to 3 days. Best served at room temperature.

$$

VANILLA CREAM PIE

Did you know that among the most frequently purchased items in grocery stores are bananas? Who would have guessed? I've been enjoying this wonderful dessert since I was ten and I still love it as much as I did then.

Serves 6 to 8

1	burrito-size flour tortilla (10-inch) *Mission®*
2	tablespoons butter, melted, *Land O'Lakes®*
2	tablespoons granulated sugar, *C&H®*
2	ripe bananas, peeled
2	containers (4 ounces each) refrigerated prepared vanilla pudding, *Jell-O®*
1	teaspoon vanilla extract, *McCormick®*
1	container (8-ounce) frozen nondairy whipped topping, thawed, *Cool Whip®*

Prep time: 15 minutes
Cooking time: 20 minutes
Set-up time: 1 hour

Preparation:

Preheat oven to 325 degrees.
Generously brush both sides of tortilla with melted butter.
Sprinkle 1 side of tortilla with sugar.
Line a 9-inch-round pie pan with tortilla, sugared side up.
Bake until tortilla is crisp and golden, about 20 minutes.
Cool crust completely.
Cut bananas crosswise into 1/4-inch-thick slices.
Mix pudding and vanilla extract in medium bowl to blend.
Fold in 1 cup whipped topping.
Fold in banana slices.
Transfer mixture to prepared tortilla crust.
Cover pie tightly and refrigerate at least 1 hour, or up to 8 hours.
Cut pie into wedges.
Top wedges with remaining whipped topping and serve.

$$

BERRY COOKIE COBBLER

This is easy, easy, easy—delicious, delicious, delicious. You'll look and feel like a professional baker when this beautiful dessert comes out of the oven. If the filling bubbles over a bit in baking, leave it (it adds a mouthwatering appeal). I let it cool just a little and serve it with a scoop of vanilla ice cream. Yum.

Serves 8

2   bags (12 ounces each) frozen mixed berries, thawed
1   container (21-ounce) apple pie filling, *Comstock®*
1/3   cup granulated sugar, *C&H®*
1 1/2   teaspoons ground cinnamon, *McCormick®*
1   roll (18-ounce) prepared sugar cookie dough, *Pillsbury®*
        Vanilla ice cream, *Dreyer's®* or *Edy's®*

Prep time: 5 minutes
Cooking time: 45 minutes

Preparation:

Preheat oven to 350 degrees.
In a large bowl, mix berries, apple pie filling, sugar, and cinnamon.
Transfer fruit mixture to an 8x8x2-inch baking dish.
Crumble cookie dough over fruit, covering thickly and completely.
Bake uncovered until cookie crust is golden and crisp, and juices bubble thickly, about
   45 minutes.
Serve warm with ice cream.

$

RICOTTA BERRY BURSTS

Make this as soon as possible! So smooth and creamy, it's packed with the most wonderful burst of berry flavor.

Serves 6

I	package (4-ounce) 6 mini graham cracker crusts, *Keebler®*
I	egg white
3/4	cup boysenberry jam, *Knott's Berry Farm®*
I	container (14-ounce) whole milk ricotta
I	tablespoon orange juice, *Minute Maid®*
	Fresh boysenberries or blackberries (optional)

Prep time: 10 minutes
Cooking time: 5 minutes

P r e p a r a t i o n :

Preheat oven to 375 degrees.
Brush crusts with egg white.
Bake until golden, about 5 minutes.
Cool crusts completely.
Melt 1/4 cup jam in a small glass bowl in microwave, about 30 seconds.
Spoon 2 teaspoons melted jam over bottom of each crust.
Blend remaining 1/2 cup jam, ricotta, and orange juice in blender until smooth.
Divide mixture among crusts.
Serve immediately or cover tightly and refrigerate up to 8 hours.
Garnish with berries (optional).

$$

CREAM CHEESE FLAN

Serves 8

1	cup granulated sugar, *C&H®*
1/4	cup water
1	can (14-ounce) sweetened condensed milk, *Carnation®*
1	package (8-ounce) cream cheese, softened, *Philadelphia®*
5	eggs
1	teaspoon vanilla extract, *McCormick®*
1	can (12-ounce) evaporated milk, *Carnation®*

Prep time: 5 minutes
Cooking time: 1 hour
Cooling time: 4 hours

P r e p a r a t i o n :

Position rack in center of oven and preheat to 350 degrees.
Arrange eight 6-ounce oven-safe custard or dessert cups in a heavy large roasting pan.
Stir sugar and water in a heavy small saucepan over low heat until sugar dissolves.
Increase heat to high and boil without stirring until liquid is a deep golden brown, brushing down sides of saucepan with a wet pastry brush to prevent sugar from crystallizing, about 12 minutes.
Quickly pour syrup into prepared cups.
In a blender, combine condensed milk, cream cheese, eggs, and vanilla.
Blend until just smooth, about 30 seconds.
Transfer to an 8-cup measuring cup or large bowl.
Whisk in evaporated milk.
Divide custard equally among prepared cups.
Transfer roasting pan to oven.
Pour enough water into roasting pan to come halfway up the sides of the custard cups.
Bake until sides are firmly set and only very center of custards jiggle slightly when cups are gently shaken, about 45 minutes (custards will firm up as they cool).
Remove cups from pan, cover tightly with aluminum foil, and refrigerate until cold, at least 4 hours and up to 24 hours.
Run small sharp knife around sides of custards.
Invert each cup onto a dessert plate, shaking gently to release custard from cups.
Drizzle caramel sauce over custard.
Serve cold.

Note: Rewarm cups in microwave to dissolve caramel sauce if necessary. Garnish flans with fresh berries if desired.

$$

GOOEY MUD PIE

Serves 8

1	jar (11.75-ounce) hot fudge topping, slightly warm, *Smucker's®*
1	9-inch premade chocolate pie crust, *Keebler®*
1	quart coffee ice cream, *Dreyer's®* or *Edy's®*
1	cup frozen light nondairy whipped topping, thawed, *Cool Whip®*
1	bottle (7.25-ounce) Magic Shell® chocolate topping, *Smucker's®*

Prep time: 20 minutes
Set-up time: 1 hour, 45 minutes

P r e p a r a t i o n :

Drizzle half of the warm fudge topping over bottom of pie crust.
Spoon half of the ice cream in an even layer over fudge topping.
Drizzle remaining fudge topping over ice cream.
Freeze pie for 15 minutes.
Using a wooden spoon, stir remaining half of ice cream in a large bowl to loosen.
Stir in 1/4 cup whipped topping.
Fold in remaining whipped topping to create a mousselike texture.
Spoon mixture onto fudge-topped ice cream layer.
Freeze until firm, at least 1 hour.
Drizzle 1/4 of the Magic Shell® over top of pie.
Freeze pie 5 minutes.
Repeat drizzling and freezing 3 more times.
Cut pie into wedges and serve immediately.

Storage and Leftovers: Cover tightly and store in freezer for up to 3 days.

$$

MARBLED SOUR CREAM CAKE

Makes 1 large bundt cake or about 8-10 servings

	Nonstick vegetable cooking spray, *PAM®*
I	cup semisweet chocolate morsels, *Hershey's®*
I	package (18.25-ounce) yellow cake mix, *Betty Crocker Super Moist®*
I	cup sour cream
I	cup water
3/4	cup vegetable oil, *Wesson®*
3/4	cup granulated sugar, *C&H®*
4	eggs

Prep time:	10 minutes
Cooking time:	55 minutes
Cooling time:	30 minutes

Preparation:

Position rack in center of oven and preheat to 375 degrees.

Spray a 10-inch (12-cup) bundt cake pan with nonstick spray.

Microwave chocolate morsels in a medium microwave-safe bowl for 30 seconds on high. Stir to blend.

Continue to microwave until morsels are melted and smooth, about 30 seconds longer. Set aside.

In a large bowl, combine all remaining ingredients.

Using an electric mixer, beat until very well blended, about 2 minutes.

Spoon 2 cups of cake batter into melted chocolate, then mix thoroughly to form chocolate batter.

Spoon chocolate batter and yellow batter alternately into prepared pan.

Bake until a toothpick inserted in center of cake comes out clean, about 55 minutes.

Transfer pan to a cooling rack and cool completely, or refrigerate for 30 minutes.

Invert cake onto a platter, then carefully remove pan.

Storage and Leftovers: Cover tightly and store at room temperature for up to 3 days.

$$

KAHLÚA® TIRAMISU

After reading all of these wonderful dessert recipes you may think I'm a spokesperson for Cool Whip®—however, I just happen to be a huge fan. The reason I like to use Cool Whip® is simple: I think it's one of the best-tasting premade products on the market and its consistency is incredible for cooking! Pure perfection for topping off my Kahlúa® Tiramisu. Serve this dessert after dinner with coffee, at an afternoon tea, or anytime, really. You're in for a wonderful treat.

Serves 6

12	teaspoons plus 2 tablespoons Kahlúa®
18	soft lady fingers (available in the packaged-baked-goods section)
1	container (8-ounce) mascarpone cheese, softened
1	tablespoon granulated sugar, *C&H®*
3	containers (4 ounces each) refrigerated prepared vanilla pudding, *Jell-O®*
6	teaspoons frozen nondairy whipped topping, thawed, *Cool Whip®*
	Cocoa powder, *Hershey's®*

Prep time: 10 minutes
Set-up time: 30 minutes

Preparation:

Line six 1-cup glass custard cups with plastic wrap.
Spoon 2 teaspoons Kahlúa® into each cup.
Soak 3 lady fingers in each cup, turning to coat both sides.
Arrange lady fingers around sides of cups. Set aside.
In a large bowl, whisk mascarpone, sugar, and remaining 2 tablespoons Kahlúa® until
   just smooth.
Whisk in pudding.
Divide pudding mixture equally among prepared cups.
Cover tightly and refrigerate until set, about 30 minutes, or up to 1 day.
Uncover cups.
Invert cups onto plates and remove plastic wrap.
Top with whipped topping and sprinkle with cocoa powder just before serving.

$$$

BANANAS FOSTER PIE

These mini Bananas Foster pies will melt in your mouth. They're sensational! Make a couple extra and save them for yourself. A few secret indulgences never hurt anyone.

Makes 12

2	packages (4 ounces each) 6 mini graham cracker crusts, *Keebler®*
1	egg white, beaten slightly
1	cup (packed) golden brown sugar, *C&H®*
1	stick butter, cut into pieces, *Land O'Lakes®*
1/4	cup brandy, *Christian Brothers®*
6	bananas, peeled and thinly sliced
	Vanilla ice cream, *Dreyer's®* or *Edy's®*
	Frozen nondairy whipped topping, thawed, *Cool Whip®*

Prep time:	13 minutes
Cooking time:	10 minutes

Preparation:

Preheat oven to 375 degrees.

Arrange pie crusts (in pie tins) on a large cookie sheet.

Brush crusts with egg white.

Bake until crusts are golden, about 5 minutes.

Whisk brown sugar and butter in a heavy medium saucepan over medium heat until butter melts and mixture is creamy, about 3 minutes.

Whisk in brandy.

Remove from heat.

Stir in bananas.

Let stand 5 minutes.

Divide banana mixture equally among pie crusts.

Serve with ice cream and whipped topping.

$

APPETIZERS AND COCKTAILS

Social soirees can be simple, elegant, and inexpensive to pull off when you use shortcuts. I have thrown many a great party—some for five guests, others for 50 guests, even one for 550 guests. And I can tell you, preparation and attitude are everything—even when you're only entertaining for two, be it a romantic gesture or catch-up time with your best friend.

With the right combination of appetizers and cocktails, your gathering will be a guaranteed success. Good food, an atmosphere of fun, and a stylish presentation are always important, but preparations don't need to be elaborate or overwhelming for the results to be tasteful. While everyone will appreciate your hard work, there is no reason why they should know you didn't labor in the kitchen for hours.

With a little organization and simple Semi-Homemade recipes, you'll have the freedom to sit back, relax, and enjoy yourself and your guests.

Appetizers and Cocktails

SESAME CHICKEN DRUMETTES

There used to be a place on the 3rd Street Promenade in Santa Monica, California that had the most amazing drumettes—that's all they served. Unbelievable, wonderful drumettes in all sorts of flavors; sesame was my favorite. When they closed shop I scrambled to create a recipe that could pass as its twin. Full of flavor, the outside is always perfectly crispy and the inside is always tender and juicy.

Serves 4

1/3	cup teriyaki sauce, *Kikkoman®*
1 1/2	tablespoons dry sherry, *Christian Brothers®*
1 1/2	tablespoons toasted sesame seeds, *Sun Luck®*
1 1/4	pounds chicken drumettes (about 12)
1 1/2	tablespoons barbecue sauce, *KC Masterpiece®*
1 1/2	tablespoons honey, *Sue Bee®*
1/4	teaspoon oriental sesame oil, *Sun Luck®*

Prep time: 35 minutes
Cooking time: 25 minutes

Preparation:

In a large resealable plastic bag, combine teriyaki sauce, sherry, and sesame seeds.
Add chicken drumettes, turning to coat.
Seal bag and refrigerate at least 30 minutes, or up to 1 day.
Preheat oven to 400 degrees.
Line a cookie sheet with foil.
Using tongs, transfer drumettes to cookie sheet. Discard marinade.
Bake until drumettes are golden brown, about 15 minutes.
Mix barbecue sauce, honey, and sesame oil in a small bowl.
Brush drumettes with honey mixture and bake 5 minutes.
Turn drumettes and brush with honey mixture and bake 5 minutes longer.
Can be served hot or at room temperature.

Storage and Leftovers: Cover tightly and store in refrigerator for up to 2 days. Reheat in a 400-degree oven for 20 minutes, or until warm.

$$

Music: *Kruder Dorfmeister, "The K & D Sessions"*

PAN-FRIED DUMPLINGS

Makes 12 dumplings

2	teaspoons soy sauce, *Kikkoman®*
1	teaspoon hot Chinese-style mustard, *Sun Luck®*
1/2	teaspoon minced fresh garlic, *McCormick®*
1/2	teaspoon oriental sesame oil, *Sun Luck®*
1	can (14-ounce) chow mein vegetables, rinsed and drained very well, *Chun King®*
24	square wonton wrappers, *Dynasty®*
1/2	cup canola oil, *Wesson®*
	Toasted white sesame seeds, *Sun Luck®*
	Black sesame seeds, *Wel-Pac®*
	For dipping: soy sauce, sweet and sour sauce, and hot Chinese-style mustard

Prep time: 15 minutes
Cooking time: 18 minutes

Preparation:

Preheat oven to 350 degrees.
Blend first 4 ingredients in a food processor.
Add vegetables.
Using on/off turns, pulse until vegetables are just minced.
Drain excess liquid from vegetable mixture.
Arrange 12 wonton wrappers on work surface.
Lightly brush edges of wrappers with water.
Spoon 1 tablespoon vegetable mixture into center of each wrapper.
Top with remaining wonton wrappers, pressing to enclose filling completely.
Using ravioli cutter or sharp knife, cut edges of wontons.
Heat canola oil in heavy large skillet over medium heat.
Working in batches, fry dumplings until just golden, about 1 minute per side.
Arrange fried dumplings, rounded side up, on a large cookie sheet.
Bake until dumplings are golden brown, about 10 minutes.
Transfer dumplings to serving tray.
Sprinkle with toasted sesame seeds.
Serve with dipping sauces.

Note: Once assembled, dumplings can be frozen and cooked as directed.

$$ Music: *Thievery Corporation, "Sounds from the Thievery for Life"*

CHORIZO TAQUITOS

My girlfriends threw the most beautiful bridal shower for me and decided to prepare all Semi-Homemade recipes that appear in this book. These taquitos were an absolute hit (as was the Black Bean Quesadilla, page 46). Both disappeared from their serving platters instantly. You're sure to get the same results when you serve them.

Makes 12 pieces

1	package (16-ounce, bulk) beef chorizo sausage, casing removed
1	cup medium chunky salsa, drained, *Pace®*
1	cup shredded mild cheddar cheese, *Kraft®*
6	fajita-size flour tortillas, *Mission®*
1	cup prepared guacamole (refrigerated section)
1/4	cup sour cream

Prep time: 15 minutes
Cooking time: 25 minutes

Preparation:

Preheat oven to 400 degrees.
In a large skillet, sauté sausage over medium heat until browned, about 6 minutes.
Drain 1/4 cup of oil from cooked sausage.
Set sausage aside to cool.
Stir salsa and cheese into sausage in skillet.
Place 1 tortilla on a clean work surface.
Spoon 1/4 cup of the sausage mixture down center of tortilla.
Fold tortilla in half, then roll up.
Secure with toothpicks.
Place on a foil-covered cookie sheet.
Repeat 5 times.
Bake until filling is hot and tortilla is crisp and golden brown, about 18 minutes.
Cut taquitos in half crosswise.
Serve hot with guacamole and sour cream.

$$

Music: *Yo-Yo Ma, Bobby McFerrin, "Hush"*

CRABMEAT CUCUMBER ROUNDS

A little exotic and very tasty, these crab-topped cucumber rounds are a refreshing change in bite-size food. Remember to wash and dry the cucumber before slicing it, and please don't peel the skin. Before slicing you may want to use a fork to create decorative lines down the side of the cucumber. This appetizer looks and tastes quite professional.

Makes 16 rounds

1/4	cup mayonnaise, *Best Foods®* or *Hellmann's®*
1	teaspoon prepared horseradish, *Morehouse®*
1/2	teaspoon Dijon mustard, *French's®*
1/2	teaspoon Worcestershire sauce, *Lea & Perrins®*
1	can (4.25-ounce) crabmeat, *Geisha®*
1/2	large unpeeled English hothouse cucumber, cut crosswise into 16 thin slices (about 1/4-inch-thick slices)
8	pimiento-stuffed green olives, sliced, *Star®*

Prep time: 15 minutes
Cooling time: 30 minutes

Preparation:

In a small bowl, mix together mayonnaise, horseradish, mustard, and Worcestershire sauce.
Stir in crabmeat.
Cover and refrigerate for 30 minutes.
Arrange cucumber slices in a single layer on a serving tray.
Spoon 1 tablespoon of crabmeat mixture onto each cucumber slice.
Garnish with olive slices and serve.

$$

Music: *Amel Larrieux, "Infinite Possibilities"*

FETA-STUFFED ARTICHOKE BOTTOMS

I have always loved to eat artichokes. When I was a child, my sister Cynthia and I would share a whole artichoke and then argue about who would get to eat the "heart," as we called it. Really it was the bottom; ultimately, we always split it. Years later Cindy and I visited the Greek island of Santorini and reminisced about our artichoke wars, while stuffing ourselves with these great Greek appetizers.

Makes 15 pieces

1/2	cup jarred roasted red bell peppers, chopped, *Progresso®*
1/4	cup chopped ripe olives (black), *Early California®*
1/4	cup crumbled feta cheese
1	tablespoon olive oil, *Bertolli®*
1	can (13 3/4-ounce) artichoke bottoms (approximately 15 pieces), drained and patted dry, *Progresso®*

Prep time: 5 minutes
Cooking time: 7 minutes

Preparation:

Preheat broiler.
Line a cookie sheet with foil.
In a medium bowl, combine peppers, olives, cheese, and olive oil.
Place artichoke bottoms on prepared cookie sheet.
Mound 1 1/2 teaspoons of stuffing on each artichoke.
Broil 7 minutes, or until golden on top.
Transfer artichokes to a platter and serve hot.

Storage and Leftovers: Cover tightly and store in refrigerator for up to 1 day.

$$

Music: *Ivy, "Apartment Life"*

ORIENTAL PORK WRAPPERS

Makes about 24

1	package (12-ounce) pork sausage, *Jimmy Dean®*
2	green onions, minced
1	tablespoon soy sauce, *Kikkoman®*
1	tablespoon hoisin sauce, *Sun Luck®*
1/2	teaspoon minced fresh garlic, *McCormick®*
24	square wonton wrappers, *Dynasty®*
	Nonstick vegetable cooking spray, *PAM®*
	For dipping: soy sauce, hoisin sauce, chili garlic sauce, and hot Chinese-style mustard

Prep time: 15 minutes
Cooking time: 25 minutes

Preparation:

In a medium bowl, mix first 5 ingredients.
Lay out 8 wonton wrappers on a clean surface and brush edges with water.
Place 1 tablespoon of pork mixture in center of each wrapper.
Gather edges of wrapper together over filling.
Press edges of wrapper together, enclosing filling completely.
Repeat with remaining wrappers and filling.
Place a collapsible metal steamer rack in a large wide pot.
Fill pot with 1/2 inch of water.
Spray steamer rack with nonstick spray.
Bring water to a simmer.
Working in batches, arrange dumplings on rack an inch apart.
Cover pot with lid and steam dumplings until cooked thoroughly, about 8 minutes.
Watch the water level and add more as needed.
Transfer dumplings to platter.
Serve with dipping sauces.

$$ Music: *Ultra Lounge, Various Artists, "Best of Collection, Volume 1"*

SMOKED SALMON AND OLIVE BLINI

Makes about 32 blini

1	cup buckwheat pancake and waffle mix, *Aunt Jemima®*
1	cup whole milk
1	egg
1	tablespoon vegetable oil, *Wesson®*
	Nonstick vegetable cooking spray, *PAM®*
6	ounces sliced smoked salmon or lox, *Vita®*
3/4	cup kalamata olive spread, *Peloponnese®*
3/4	cup light sour cream
	Fresh dill, chopped
	Chopped ripe olives (black), *Early California®*

Prep time:	15 minutes
Cooking time:	10 minutes

Preparation:

In a medium bowl, stir pancake mix, milk, egg, and oil until just blended. Set aside.
Spray griddle with nonstick spray.
Heat griddle over medium low heat.
Spoon several 1-tablespoon dollops of batter onto griddle.
Cook for 2 minutes, or until bubbles appear, then turn blini over and cook for
   1 minute. Set aside.
Cut salmon or lox into 32 equal pieces.
Place blini on a platter.
Spread each blini with 1 teaspoon of the olive spread.
Top with a piece of smoked salmon, then with 1 teaspoon of sour cream.
Sprinkle with dill and chopped black olives.

$$ Music: *Ultra Lounge, Various Artists, "Best of Collection, Volume II"*

ITALIAN FONDUE

I love to make this and serve it as individual fondues to pass. When entertaining, serve alongside dinner rolls for an extra special touch. They're adorable, delicious, unique, and your guests will be amazed at your creative attention to detail.

Serves 6

2	tablespoons butter, *Land O'Lakes®*
2	tablespoons fresh sage, finely chopped
2	tablespoons all-purpose flour, *Pillsbury®*
1 1/4	cups dry white wine, *Vendage®*
1	jar (16-ounce) Alfredo sauce, *Classico®*
1	package (8-ounce) shredded Six-Cheese Italian Blend (mozzarella, smoked provolone, Parmesan, Romano, Fontina, and Asiago cheeses), *Sargento®*
	Dippers: crusty Italian bread, cubed; quartered figs; and cooked, cubed potatoes

Prep time: 5 minutes
Cooking time: 10 minutes

Preparation:

Melt butter in a heavy large saucepan over medium heat.
Add sage and cook until butter is golden brown, about 2 minutes.
Whisk in flour and cook for 1 minute.
Whisk in wine and simmer for 2 minutes.
Whisk in Alfredo sauce.
Gradually add cheese, whisking until cheese melts and mixture is smooth.
Transfer mixture to a fondue pot, chafing dish, or ceramic bowl.
Serve with bread, figs, and potatoes.

$$ Music: *ABBA, "The Best of ABBA"*

FIESTA FONDUE

For sure fondue is back. There are restaurants whose entire menus consist of different kinds of fondue. Hard to imagine there's such a demand that fondue alone could keep a place in business, but there is—which is why I've included so many variations for you to choose from. Simple to make, this dish always gets glowing reviews.

Serves 6

1	can (10 3/4-ounce) cheddar cheese soup, *Campbell's®*
1	package (8-ounce) shredded sharp cheddar cheese, *Kraft®*
1	cup chunky chipotle salsa, *Pace®*
1	cup whole milk
	Dippers: french bread, cubed; jicama sticks; corn tortilla chips; and warm flour tortillas

Prep time: 5 minutes
Cooking time: 10 minutes

Preparation:

Stir all ingredients except dippers in a heavy medium saucepan over medium heat until shredded cheese melts and mixture is smooth.
Transfer mixture to a fondue pot, chafing dish, or ceramic bowl.
Serve with bread, jicama, tortilla chips, and tortillas.

$

Music: *Supreme Beings of Leisure, Self-Titled*

WHITE CHOCOLATE FONDUE

White-chocolate-covered strawberries—people pay a fortune for these delicacies, but you can create the same thing, if not better, with this sure-fire recipe. But don't stop with dipping strawberries. Ten years ago I found Ruffles® ridged potato chips to be wonderful dipped in chocolate: the salt and chocolate are great together. Recently, high-end stores and catalogues began selling chocolate-covered potato chips for a small fortune. I should have cashed in on these chips myself! What's your favorite food to dip? (See page 204.)

Serves 6

1	cup heavy cream
1/2	stick unsalted butter, *Land O'Lakes®*
2	packages (12 ounces each) premier white morsels, *Nestlé®*
	Dippers: sliced apples, bananas, strawberries, crisp cookies, pretzels, and cubed pound cake, *Sara Lee®*

Prep time:	3 minutes
Cooking time:	7 minutes

Preparation:

In a large saucepan over medium heat, combine cream and butter.
Bring mixture to a simmer, stirring constantly.
Remove pan from heat.
Add white morsels.
Stir until melted and smooth.
Cool slightly.
Transfer to a fondue pot, chafing dish, or ceramic bowl.
Serve with apples, bananas, strawberries, cookies, pretzels, and pound cake.

$$ Music: *That Guitar Man from Central Park, "The People on the Hill"*

BEER MARGARITAS

Arriba, arriba! These Beer Margaritas will be gone in no time. You may as well double the recipe because everyone will want seconds.

Serves 4

1	lime, cut into 8 wedges
1/4	cup coarse salt
2	bottles (12 ounces each) *Corona®* or your favorite beer, chilled
1/2	cup frozen concentrate limeade, thawed, *Minute Maid®*
1/2	cup chilled tequila, *Jose Cuervo Especial®*
	Ice cubes

Prep time: 2 minutes

Preparation:

Rub lime wedges around rims of 4 margarita glasses.
Dip rims into salt to coat lightly.
In a medium pitcher, combine beer, limeade, and tequila.
Fill prepared glasses with ice, then with margarita mixture.
Garnish with remaining lime wedges.
Serve immediately.

$

Music Selection: *Moby, "Play"*

RASPBERRY SAKE

A hot new sushi place opened up down the street from my husband's office. While waiting there for him one evening, I had a quick drink—infused sake. Everyone around me was raving about it, and now so am I. The infusion method is difficult and time-consuming, so here's my shortcut to getting a similar flavor.

Serves 6

1	bottle (750 ml) sake, chilled, *Gekkeikan*®
1	pint (16 ounces) canned wild berry juice cocktail concentrate, chilled, *Welch's*®
1	cup crushed ice
1/2	cup frozen raspberries, thawed
1/4	cup fresh lemon juice, or *ReaLemon*®

Prep time: 5 minutes

Preparation:

In a blender, combine sake, wild berry juice, ice, raspberries, and lemon juice.
Pulse several times until raspberries are completely crushed.
Strain into 6 martini glasses.
Serve immediately.

$$

Music Selection: *k.d. lang, "Invincible Summer"*

GIN PLUSH

Serves 1

4	ice cubes
1/3	cup gin, *Tanqueray®*
1/4	cup guava nectar, *Kern's®*
1/4	cup pineapple juice, *Dole®*
1/4	cup orange juice, *Minute Maid®*
1/4	cup club soda, chilled, *Canada Dry®*

Prep time: 1 minute

Preparation: Place ice cubes and all ingredients in a large cocktail glass. Serve immediately.

$$

CHAMPAGNE PUNCH

Serves 6

1	can (20-ounce) crushed pineapple in heavy syrup, *Dole®*
1	cup fresh lemon juice, or *ReaLemon®*
1	cup maraschino cherry juice, *Red Star®*
1	cup dark rum, *Myers's®*
1/2	cup brandy, *Christian Brothers®*
1	bottle (750 ml) chilled brute champagne, *Korbel®*

Prep time: 5 minutes
Cooling time: 30 minutes

Preparation: In a large punch bowl or pitcher, stir pineapple, lemon juice, cherry juice, rum, and brandy to blend. Refrigerate for 30 minutes. Add champagne just before serving.

$$$

SOUR APPLE MARTINI

Serves 1

4	ice cubes
3	tablespoons apple sourball mix, *Hiram Walker®*
3	tablespoons vodka, *Smirnoff®*
2	teaspoons sweet vermouth
1	apple slice

Prep time: 2 minutes

Preparation: In a cocktail shaker, combine all ingredients except the apple slice. Cover and shake for 15 seconds. Strain into a martini glass and garnish with the apple slice. Serve immediately.

$$

CUBANA RUM

Serves 1

1/3	cup apricot nectar, *Kern's®*
1/4	cup lime juice, or *Rose's Lime Juice®*
1/4	cup apricot brandy, *Hiram Walker®*
1/4	cup light rum, *Bacardi®*
4	ice cubes

Prep time: 5 minutes

Preparation: Combine all ingredients in a cocktail shaker. Cover and shake for 15 seconds. Strain into a glass and serve immediately.

$$

Music: *Bette Midler, "Bette"*

Clockwise from lower right: Gin Plush, Champagne Punch, Cubana Rum, Sour Apple Martini

SASSY SANGRIA

Great for a brunch or just a bunch, these sassy sangrias carry a powerful punch—careful or you'll be singing the latest Gypsy Kings CD yourself.

Makes 8 drinks

3	cups chianti, *Villa Antinori*®
1	cup brandy, *Christian Brothers*®
1/4	cup triple sec, *Hiram Walker*®
1	orange, sliced
1	lime, sliced
1	lemon, sliced
1	apple, cored and diced
8	fresh raspberries
2	cups club soda, chilled, *Schweppes*®

Prep time: 8 minutes
Cooling time: 3 hours

Preparation:

In a large pitcher, combine all ingredients except club soda.
Cover tightly and refrigerate 3 hours.
Pour 3/4 cup sangria mixture and 1/4 cup club soda into each glass, dividing fruit equally.
Serve immediately.

$$ Music: *Gypsy Kings, "The Best of the Gypsy Kings"*

139

cocktails

BERRY SMOOTH

Serves 4

2	cups chilled lemonade, *Minute Maid®*
1/2	cup cassis liqueur, *Hiram Walker®, or* blackberry brandy, *Hiram Walker®*
1/2	cup vodka, *Smirnoff®*
2	tablespoons lime juice, or sweetened lime juice, *Rose's®*
2	cups ice cubes

Prep time: 3 minutes

Preparation: In a pitcher, stir all ingredients except ice. Fill glasses with ice, then with equal portions lemonade mixture. Serve immediately.

$$

SHERRY FRUIT BOWL

Serves 6

1	container (16-ounce) frozen sweetened sliced strawberries, thawed
1	can (15-ounce) sliced peaches (with juice), *S&W®*
1	cup dry sherry or madeira, *Paul Masson®*
1	bottle (750 ml) chilled chardonnay, *Vendage®*

Prep time: 5 minutes
Cooling time: 1 hour

Preparation: In a punch bowl or pitcher, stir strawberries (with syrup), peaches (with juice), and sherry or madeira. Refrigerate for 1 hour. Stir in wine and serve immediately.

$$

COOL RED WINE

Serves 6

1	bottle (750 ml) chilled beaujolais, *Louis Jadot®*
1	can (15-ounce) sliced peaches in heavy syrup, *Del Monte®*
1	orange, sliced
1/2	cup *Cointreau®*
1/2	cup orange juice, *Minute Maid®*
1/4	cup granulated sugar, *C&H®*

Prep time: 5 minutes
Cooling time: 1 hour

Preparation: Stir all ingredients in a large pitcher. Cover tightly and refrigerate for 1 hour. Fill glasses with equal portions of red wine mixture. Serve immediately.

$$

SCARLET O'BRANDY

Serves 1

1	cup crushed ice
1/3	cup *Southern Comfort®*
1/3	cup cranberry juice cocktail, *Ocean Spray®*
2	tablespoons fresh lime juice, or sweetened lime juice, *Rose's®*
1	orange wedge

Prep time: 2 minutes

Preparation: Combine all ingredients except orange wedge in cocktail shaker. Cover and shake for 15 seconds. Strain into glass and garnish with orange wedge. Serve immediately.

$$

Music: *Craig David, "Born to Do It"*
Clockwise from lower right: Berry Smooth, Sherry Fruit Bowl, Cool Red Wine, Scarlet O'Brandy

SOUPS AND SALADS

Served as a snack, light lunch, side dish, or main meal, soups and salads are always welcome. The savviest of chefs know that soups and salads as stand-alones or as starters to a main course are foolproof ways to ensure a successful meal. Who doesn't love to have a fresh, crisp salad? Or a steaming bowl of flavorful soup? Both are staples of any diet.

Soups and salads are a tasty and easy way to get your daily requirements of nutrients and vitamins. They're also among the quickest courses to create. Those of us who are watching our diets can look forward to soups and salads as satisfying, low-calorie feasts.

By adding the smallest accoutrements, you can change the flavor, texture, and presentation of your soup or salad. Garnishes as simple as toasted almonds, sweet candied walnuts, a dollop of cumin-flavored sour cream, or a decorative piece of puff pastry are easy to add and a great way to show off your culinary creativity.

Soups and Salads

CRABBY BISQUE

This is a soup among soups. Not much compares to this flavorful Crabby Bisque. This "must make" is super to serve in coffee mugs and makes the most unique appetizer.

Serves 2

I	can (10 1/2-ounce) restaurant-style condensed crab bisque, *Bookbinder's®*
3/4	cup plus 2 tablespoons heavy cream
I	tablespoon fresh parsley, chopped
I	can (4.25-ounce) crabmeat, *Geisha®*
I	tablespoon fresh lemon juice, or *ReaLemon®*
	Salt and cayenne pepper

Prep time:	5 minutes
Cooking time:	6 minutes

Preparation:

In a medium saucepan, combine bisque, heavy cream, and parsley.
Bring to a boil.
Stir in crabmeat with juices.
Bring to a simmer.
Add lemon juice.
Season soup to taste with salt and cayenne pepper.
Divide soup between 2 bowls.
Add I tablespoon of cream to each bowl, swirl with butter knife to create design,
    and serve.

Storage and Leftovers: Cover tightly and store in refrigerator for up to 1 day. Reheat in a saucepan over low heat, stirring frequently until warm.

$$

GOLDEN MUSHROOM SOUP

When my girlfriend Barbara describes something she thinks is amazing, she says it's "beyond." And as Barbara would say, this soup is "beyond." It's that good. So double the recipe to be sure there's enough to go around a second time—you'll need it.

Serves 2

2	tablespoons olive oil, *Bertolli*®
I	large, fresh portobello mushroom, gills scraped off and mushroom finely chopped
I	can (10 3/4-ounce) condensed golden mushroom soup, *Campbell's*®
I	cup water
3/4	cup heavy cream
I	teaspoon minced fresh garlic, *McCormick*®

Prep time: 5 minutes
Cooking time: 10 minutes

Preparation:

In a large saucepan over medium high heat, warm olive oil.
Sauté mushroom until tender, about 2 minutes.
Mix in soup, water, cream, and garlic.
Bring soup to a simmer, stirring occasionally, about 5 minutes.
Ladle soup into 2 bowls and serve.

Note: Garnish with a slice of white mushroom and herb of choice (optional).
Storage and Leftovers: Cover tightly and store in refrigerator for up to 3 days. Reheat in a saucepan
  over low heat, stirring frequently until warm.

$$

CHEDDAR POTATO SOUP

Cheez Whiz® again! I may have been able to get away with using Cheez Whiz® in one recipe, but three? (See pages 37 and 61.) I'm sure a professional foodie is bound to suggest I be sent to "culinary jail" for this. For those of you out there questioning my use of Cheese Whiz®, or even turning your nose up a bit: Don't be so quick to judge and dismiss. This soup is super and sure to please the taste buds of any cheese aficionado.

Serves 4

2	packages (11 1/2 ounces each) frozen potatoes au gratin, *Stouffer's®*
2	cups whole milk
1/4	cup Cheez Whiz®, *Kraft®*
3/4	cup shredded sharp cheddar cheese, *Kraft®*
1/2	cup green onions, chopped

Prep time: 5 minutes
Cooking time: 12 minutes

Preparation:

Prepare potatoes in microwave according to package instructions.
Whisk milk and Cheez Whiz® in a heavy large saucepan to blend.
Gently stir in scalloped potatoes.
Bring mixture to a simmer over medium heat.
Ladle soup equally into 4 bowls.
Sprinkle generously with shredded cheese and green onions.
Serve hot.

Storage and Leftovers: Cover tightly and store in refrigerator for up to 3 days. To reheat, combine Cheddar Potato Soup and 1/4 cup whole milk in a saucepan over medium heat, stirring constantly until warm.

$$

SANTE FE FIVE-BEAN SOUP

Serves 8

1	can (15-ounce) each of black beans, kidney beans, garbanzo beans, red beans, and navy (or white) beans, all drained, *S&W®*
1	can (14 1/2-ounce) chopped tomatoes, *Del Monte®*
1	can (14-ounce) chicken broth, *Swanson®*
3/4	cup chunky salsa, *Pace®*
2	teaspoons ground cumin, *McCormick®*
1	teaspoon dried red pepper flakes, *McCormick®*
1/2	cup light sour cream
1	cup chopped onions

Prep time: 8 minutes
Cooking time: 10 minutes

P r e p a r a t i o n :

Place black beans in a blender and blend until pureed.
In a large pot, stir all remaining beans, tomatoes, broth, salsa, cumin, and red pepper flakes.
Stir in pureed black beans.
Cover and simmer for 10 minutes, stirring occasionally, until hot.
Ladle soup into bowls.
Garnish with sour cream and onions.
Serve hot.

Note: For a smoother texture, entire soup can be pureed. Pureed soup can be chilled and used as a dip for chips, vegetables, or for a sauce to be served with rice.
Storage and Leftovers: Cover tightly and store in refrigerator for up to 3 days. Reheat in a saucepan over medium heat, stirring frequently until warm.

$$

CREAMY CURRIED CARROT SOUP

Serves 6

1	tablespoon vegetable oil, *Wesson®*
2	packages (8 ounces each) shredded carrots, rinsed and drained, *Ready Pac®*
1	small onion, chopped
2	teaspoons minced fresh garlic, *McCormick®*
1	tablespoon curry powder, *McCormick®*
1	can (14-ounce) chicken broth, *Swanson®*
2/3	cup whole milk
2/3	cup heavy cream
	Salt and pepper
	Plain yogurt, *Dannon®*
	Fresh cilantro, chopped

Prep time: 10 minutes
Cooking time: 18 minutes

Preparation:

Heat oil in a heavy large pot over medium heat.
Add carrots, onion, garlic, and curry powder.
Sauté until onion is tender, about 2 minutes.
Add broth, milk, and cream.
Simmer until carrots are tender, stirring occasionally, about 15 minutes.
Working in batches, puree carrot mixture in a blender until smooth.
Return soup to pot.
Season to taste with salt and pepper.
Ladle soup into bowls. Garnish with yogurt and cilantro.
Serve hot.

Note: Soup can also be chilled and served cold.
Storage and Leftovers: Cover tightly and store in refrigerator for up to 3 days. Reheat in a saucepan
  over low heat, stirring frequently until warm.

$$

BAY SHRIMP AND AVOCADO SALAD

Avocados are the best—but have you ever tried to grow an avocado tree with a pit, a couple of toothpicks, and a shallow dish of water? Impossible! Whoever thought this one up is still getting a good laugh. But laughs will not be what you get when you serve this sensational salad.

Serves 2

8	ounces fresh bay shrimp
1	cup shredded carrots, rinsed and drained, *Ready Pac®*
1/2	cup frozen petite peas, thawed, *Green Giant®*
1/2	cup frozen cut corn kernels, thawed, *Green Giant®*
4	tablespoons champagne vinaigrette, *Girards®*
	Salt and pepper
1	firm, ripe avocado, halved and pitted

Prep time: 5 minutes

Preparation:

Toss shrimp, carrots, peas, corn, and 3 tablespoons vinaigrette in a medium bowl to coat.
Season shrimp salad to taste with salt and pepper.
Place 1 avocado half on each of two plates.
Divide shrimp salad on top of avocado halves.
Drizzle the remaining 1 tablespoon of vinaigrette over avocado halves and serve.

$$

APPLE SLAW

Amazingly easy! Amazingly good! This Apple Slaw breathes new life into old coleslaw. It's tangy, with a hint of sweetness. You'll want to share this recipe with everyone you know.

Serves 4

3/4	cup sour cream
1/4	cup granulated sugar, *C&H*®
3	tablespoons apple cider vinegar, *Heinz*®
2	tablespoons ranch seasoning and salad dressing mix, *Hidden Valley*®
1	package (8-ounce) shredded cabbage and carrots, *Ready Pac*®
3	green apples, cored and diced
4	green onions, thinly sliced
	Salt and pepper

Prep time: 10 minutes
Cooling time: 20 minutes

Preparation:

Whisk sour cream, sugar, vinegar, and ranch seasoning in a large bowl to blend.
Add cabbage mixture, apples, and green onions.
Toss to coat.
Season to taste with salt and pepper.
Cover tightly and chill 20 minutes or up to 4 hours.
Serve cold.

$$

CANDIED WALNUT BUTTER SALAD

Serves 4

CANDIED WALNUTS:
	Nonstick vegetable cooking spray, *PAM®*
4	tablespoons granulated sugar, *C&H®*
1	tablespoon orange-tangerine juice, *Minute Maid®*
1	cup walnut halves, *Diamond®*
1/4	teaspoon ground cinnamon, *McCormick®*

SALAD:
2	heads butter lettuce, washed and drained
1	can (8-ounce) mandarin orange segments, drained, *Del Monte®*
1/4	red onion, very thinly sliced
1/2	cup purchased Asian-style salad dressing (such as miso dressing or ginger dressing)

Prep time: 8 minutes
Cooking time: 12 minutes

Candied Walnut Preparation:

Preheat oven to 375 degrees.

Line a large cookie sheet with foil and spray with nonstick spray.

In a 10-inch skillet over medium heat, add 3 tablespoons sugar and orange-tangerine juice.

Bring to a simmer, then add walnuts.

Cook until sugar is absorbed and mixture starts to caramelize around walnuts, stirring constantly, about 2 minutes.

In a small bowl, mix cinnamon and remaining 1 tablespoon sugar.

Toss walnuts in cinnamon-sugar.

Place walnuts in single layer on prepared cookie sheet.

Bake until walnuts appear crystallized and toasted, about 8 minutes. Set aside.

Salad Preparation:

Place 4 to 6 lettuce leaves on each plate.

Randomly place orange segments, onion slices, and walnuts on top of each lettuce bed.

Drizzle 2 tablespoons of dressing on top of each salad and serve.

$$

EGGY POTATO SALAD

Potato salad is a very personal thing. I've never run across anyone who doesn't have an opinion about how potato salad should be made. This Eggy Potato Salad has always been well received, even raved about—but if you're not an egg lover, simply omit them—you won't compromise the recipe, you'll just have a great eggless potato salad.

Serves 2

1/3	cup green onions, chopped
1/4	cup celery, finely chopped
1/4	cup mayonnaise, *Best Foods® or Hellmann's®*
2	teaspoons prepared yellow mustard, *French's®*
1	teaspoon sweet pickle relish, *Del Monte®*
2	hard-boiled eggs (refrigerated or deli section), chopped
1	can (14 1/2-ounce) sliced new potatoes, rinsed and drained, *Del Monte®*
	Salt and pepper

Prep time: 10 minutes
Cooling time: 30 minutes

Preparation:

Stir green onions, celery, mayonnaise, mustard, and relish in a medium bowl to blend.
Stir in eggs.
Fold in potatoes.
Cover tightly and refrigerate salad 30 minutes or up to 1 day.
Season to taste with salt and pepper before serving.

$$

SPICY CRAB SALAD

This salad is a meal in itself. As good as it looks, it tastes even better. It can be made ahead and easily stored for serving later. If there's any extra, don't throw it out—this salad is a scrumptious leftover (even if there are only a few bites left).

Serves 2

3	tablespoons mayonnaise, *Best Foods®* or *Hellmann's®*
1	tablespoon fresh lemon juice, or *ReaLemon®*
1	tablespoon *Chef Paul Prudhomme's Seafood Magic Seasoning Blend®*
1	tablespoon red wine vinegar, *Heinz®*
1	cup cooked white rice (1/4 cup uncooked rice), *Minute® Rice*
1	can (4.25-ounce) crabmeat, *Geisha®*
3	tablespoons sliced ripe olives (black), *Early California®*
4	small green olives, sliced, *Star®*
1	small tomato, diced
10	thin asparagus spears, trimmed and cut into 1/2-inch pieces, (lightly steamed, if desired)
	Salt and pepper
	Fresh basil leaves (optional)

Prep time: 10 minutes
Cooling time: 15 minutes

Preparation:

In a large bowl, whisk mayonnaise, lemon juice, seafood seasoning, and vinegar to blend.
Add rice, crabmeat, and olives.
Toss gently to blend.
Fold in tomato and asparagus.
Cover and refrigerate for 15 minutes.
Season to taste with salt and pepper before serving.
Garnish with fresh basil leaves (optional).

$$

PASTA GAZPACHO SALAD

I eat gazpacho year round. I adore the flavor and find it completely refreshing. Now that I'm creating new ideas for Italian food—which my husband could eat 365 days a year—this just made my life easier. Terrific, only 364 more Italian dishes to go.

Serves 4

2	packages (7 ounces each) mini-cheese ravioli, *Buitoni®*
I	large cucumber, peeled, seeded, and cubed
I	jar (24-ounce) mild chunky salsa, *Pace®*
1/2	cup fresh cilantro, chopped
1/4	cup extra-virgin olive oil, *Bertolli®*

Prep time:	15 minutes
Cooking time:	3 minutes
Cooling time:	30 minutes

Preparation:

Prepare ravioli according to package instructions. Drain.
Rinse ravioli under cold water to cool.
Combine cucumber, salsa, cilantro, and oil in large bowl.
Add cooled ravioli and toss to coat.
Refrigerate for 30 minutes before serving.

$$

$$

SNACKS

Snacking is a great American pastime, in fact, a recent *USA Today* Snapshot® poll asking "Where do you like to snack?" found that over **80** percent of us prefer to snack *at home*. This is why it's so important to be creative with our noshing foods. Most of us tend to feel a bit guilty about snacking between meals—however, it's been proven that eating certain foods between meals is actually good for us and can ultimately reduce the total amount of food that we consume. This is especially important for high-energy people, people with weight issues, and growing children.

Snacks are perfect energy boosters for kids at the end of the school day and before homework or chores. Snacks can add fun when bringing the family together to watch television or to play a board game. They can provide comfort on a cold winter's day and relief on a hot summer's day. Snacks are ideal to serve to friends and family who stop by, and great for boosting camaraderie among coworkers at the office.

Snacks

CARAMEL POPCORN

So sweet and crunchy, this popcorn will be gobbled up before the bowl hits the table. At our house we get individual bowls so everyone is assured of getting a fair share. A great gift to give in bags or tins. Don't be surprised if you get calls for the recipe. Everyone loves homemade goodies.

Makes about 10 cups

	Nonstick vegetable cooking spray, *PAM®*
3	bags (2.85 ounces each) microwave popcorn (no salt or butter), *Newman's Own®*
1	stick butter, *Land O'Lakes®*
1	cup (packed) golden brown sugar, *C&H®*
2/3	cup light corn syrup, *Karo®*
1	teaspoon baking soda, *Arm & Hammer®*

Prep time   5 minutes
Cooking time: 1 hour
Cooling time: 20 minutes

P r e p a r a t i o n :

Preheat oven to 300 degrees.
Spray 2 large cookie sheets with nonstick spray.
Microwave popcorn according to package instructions.
Place popcorn in a very large bowl or roasting pan. Set aside.
In a 2-quart saucepan over medium heat, stir the butter, sugar, and corn syrup until
    butter is melted and sugar dissolves.
Bring to a boil and cook 4 minutes without stirring.
Remove from heat and add baking soda to caramel sauce (mixture will foam).
Drizzle caramel sauce evenly over popcorn.
Using two wooden spoons, toss popcorn to coat evenly with caramel sauce (popcorn
    will deflate somewhat).
Spread caramel corn in an even layer onto each prepared cookie sheet.
Bake until caramel corn is almost crisp, stirring every 15 minutes, for a total of
    45 minutes. (Rotate pans halfway through baking.)
Using a metal spatula, loosen caramel corn from cookie sheets.
Cool caramel corn completely.

Storage and Leftovers: Store in an airtight container at room temperature for up to 7 days.

$

TORTELLONI AND RAVIOLI BITES

Serves 10

1	package (9-ounce) assorted tortelloni (refrigerated section), *Buitoni®*
1	package (9-ounce) assorted ravioli (refrigerated section), *Buitoni®*
1	container (7-ounce) pesto sauce, *Buitoni®*
1	container (10-ounce) Alfredo sauce, *Buitoni®*
	Skewers or toothpicks

Prep time: 5 minutes
Cooking time: 5 minutes

P r e p a r a t i o n : Prepare tortelloni and ravioli according to package instructions. Arrange both pastas on the same platter in a decorative fashion (by color or shape). Heat pesto and Alfredo sauces separately and serve on the side. Serve pasta with toothpicks or small skewers for dipping into sauces.

$$

HEALTHY ONION RINGS

Serves 4

	Nonstick vegetable cooking spray, *PAM®*
1	large onion
1 1/4	cups Italian style bread crumbs, *Progresso®*
1/2	teaspoon minced fresh garlic, *McCormick®*
1	cup low-fat milk
1	cup all-purpose flour, *Pillsbury®*
3	large egg whites, beaten slightly

Prep time: 8 minutes
Cooking time: 30 minutes

P r e p a r a t i o n : Preheat oven to 400 degrees. Spray 2 large cookie sheets with nonstick spray. Cut onion into 1/2-inch-thick slices. Separate slices into rings. In a small bowl, combine bread crumbs and garlic. Set aside. Place milk, flour, and egg whites into three separate small bowls. Dip each onion ring into milk, flour, egg white, and bread crumbs (in that order). Place on prepared cookie sheets and bake for 20 minutes. Turn onion rings over and bake until golden brown, about 10 minutes longer.

$$

MINI BISCUIT PIZZAS

Mini pizzas are always popular—they make fantastic finger food for family and friends. Fun to make and a quick cleanup, they're great for after-school snacks, rainy day treats, or as just a little something to tide you over.

Serves 6

3	packages refrigerated prepared buttermilk biscuits, *Pillsbury®*
	Nonstick vegetable cooking spray, *PAM®*
1	cup onion, chopped
1	package (3-ounce) thinly sliced prosciutto (deli section), chopped, *Citterio®*
1	cup traditional tomato sauce, *Ragú®*
6	large button mushrooms, sliced
1	cup shredded pizza-blend cheese, *Sargento®*

Prep time: 10 minutes
Cooking time: 20 minutes

Preparation:

Bake biscuits according to package instructions.
Cool biscuits.
Spray cookie sheet with nonstick spray.
Split biscuits in half and arrange, split side up, on a cookie sheet. Set aside.
Bring oven heat to 400 degrees.
In a small bowl, combine onion and prosciutto.
In a second small bowl, combine tomato sauce and mushrooms.
Spread tomato mixture evenly over biscuit halves.
Sprinkle with cheese.
Top with prosciutto and onion mixture.
Bake for 12 minutes, or until topping is golden brown.
Serve warm.

$$

BAGEL CHIP DIP

Serves 6

1	container (16-ounce) sour cream
1	cup green onions, finely chopped
3/4	cup mayonnaise, *Best Foods®* or *Hellmann's®*
1/4	cup fresh parsley, chopped
3	tablespoons fresh dill, chopped
2	teaspoons seasoned salt, *Lawry's®*
2	bags bagel chips, *Bagel Crisps®*

Prep time: 5 minutes

P r e p a r a t i o n : In a medium bowl, stir all ingredients except bagel chips to blend. Serve dip with bagel chips.

Storage and Leftovers: Cover tightly and store Chip Dip in refrigerator for up to 2 days.

$

BANANA GRAPE-NUTS® CHEWS

Makes about 24 cookies

	Nonstick vegetable cooking spray, *PAM®*
6	tablespoons (3/4 stick) butter, *Land O'Lakes®*
1/3	cup (packed) golden brown sugar, *C&H®*
2	teaspoons ground cinnamon, *McCormick®*
2	egg yolks
1 1/2	cups banana quick bread mix, *Betty Crocker®*
1	cup Grape-Nuts® cereal, *Post®*
2	bananas, peeled and coarsely mashed (about 1 cup)

Prep time: 10 minutes
Cooking time: 12 minutes

P r e p a r a t i o n : Position rack in center of oven and preheat to 375 degrees. Spray large cookie sheet with nonstick spray. Using an electric mixer, beat butter, brown sugar, and cinnamon in large bowl until fluffy. Beat in yolks 1 at a time. Add quick bread mix and cereal and beat until just blended. Add mashed bananas and beat just to incorporate. Working in batches, spoon 2 tablespoons batter for each cookie onto prepared cookie sheet, spacing evenly and forming 6 mounds. Bake until cookies are golden brown on bottom and set in the middle, about 12 minutes. Using a spatula, transfer cookies to cooling rack.

Storage and Leftovers: Cover tightly and store at room temperature for up to 3 days.

$$

HUMMUS PITAS

Until now I'd never tasted a hummus I liked. In fact, before this recipe I would have sworn to you I hated hummus—but no more. This particular combination is delicious: If you're already a hummus fan, you'll be thrilled; if you're hesitant, this will surely win your heart.

Serves 4

4	pita pockets, each cut into four wedges, *Mr. Pita®*
	Olive oil cooking spray, *PAM®*
	Salt and pepper
1	large garlic clove
1	can (15 1/2-ounce) garbanzo beans, drained, *S&W®*
3	tablespoons sour cream
3	tablespoons fresh lemon juice or *ReaLemon®*
1/2	teaspoon salt
1/4	teaspoon ground cumin, *McCormick®*
1/4	cup extra-virgin olive oil, *Bertolli®*

Prep time: 8 minutes
Cooking time: 10 minutes

P r e p a r a t i o n : Preheat oven to 400 degrees. Arrange pita wedges in a single layer on a large cookie sheet. Spray wedges generously with olive oil cooking spray. Sprinkle with salt and pepper. Bake 5 minutes. Turn wedges over. Spray wedges again with olive oil cooking spray. Bake until wedges are golden brown and crisp, about 5 minutes longer. Cool completely. Meanwhile, finely mince garlic in work bowl of a food processor. Add beans, sour cream, lemon juice, salt, and cumin. Process until almost smooth. With machine running, gradually add oil through feed tube. Process until mixture is smooth, scraping down sides of work bowl occasionally. Transfer hummus to bowl. Serve with pita chips.

Storage and Leftovers: Cover hummus tightly and store in refrigerator for up to 2 days. Bake fresh pita wedges when reserving.

$

BURSTING BLUEBERRY SNACKS

Makes 8

1	bag (16-ounce) frozen unsweetened blueberries, thawed
1/2	cup pitted dates, *Sun-Maid®*
1	cup Grape-Nuts cereal, *Post®*
2	large ripe bananas, peeled and sliced
1/2	cup raisins, *Sun-Maid®*

Prep time: 10 minutes
Cooling time: 3 hours

P r e p a r a t i o n : Place blueberries in a blender and pulse for 1 minute. Gradually add dates and blend until almost smooth. In each of eight 6-ounce custard cups or glass bowls, add 2 tablespoons cereal to line bottom. Spoon 3 tablespoons blueberry mixture into each cup. Arrange sliced bananas on top of mixture. Sprinkle with raisins. Cover with remainder of blueberry mixture. Freeze 1 hour. Run small sharp knife around cups to loosen fruit mixture. Invert cups onto plates and serve.

$$

STUFFED CRESCENTS

Makes 8

1	container (8-ounce) refrigerated prepared crescent roll dough, *Pillsbury®*
4	tablespoons shredded sharp cheddar cheese, *Kraft®*
6	tablespoons shredded Parmesan cheese, *Kraft®*
4	tablespoons onion-flavored cheese spread, *Boursin®*

Prep time: 10 minutes
Cooking time: 20 minutes

P r e p a r a t i o n : Preheat oven to 350 degrees. Lay dough for each crescent roll flat on a clean surface. Fill each of 2 rolls with 2 tablespoons cheddar cheese, each of 2 rolls with 3 tablespoons Parmesan cheese, each of 2 rolls with 2 tablespoons cheese spread. Roll up each crescent to enclose filling. Place seam side down on a cookie sheet. Bake for approximately 20 minutes, or until cooked thoroughly and golden on top. Cut each roll in half and serve hot.

$$

GRAVIES AND SAUCES

Have you ever wondered how to change the flavor of an ordinary meal? How about fixing the taste of something you've overcooked? Are you bored with meatloaf and pasta? Does one more night of "rubber chicken" make you want to go squawking out of the kitchen? Before you fly the coop, you should know that I am an expert at livening up the old standbys. What is the answer? Gravies and sauces. Many people find making a gravy or sauce to be a challenge, but I have learned it's the easiest thing to do with a little know-how. My family lovingly dubbed me the "Gravy Queen." I can show you how to camouflage any imperfection, whether it's in presentation or taste.

I will share with you the secrets to giving the old food you fancy a new flavor. Whether you are serving red meat, fish, poultry, or pasta, you'll find a recipe that will make any dish delicious.

Gravies and Sauces

CREAMY MUSTARD SAUCE

Near my house is a small French café called La Conversation. In the evening they serve pork roast smothered in a mustard-based sauce. I eat every bite—it's so good. Since they won't share their secret recipe, I've created a similar sauce. I know you'll enjoy it and want to put it on any meat, fish, or foul.

Makes 1 1/2 cups

1	cup heavy cream
1/2	cup Dijon mustard, *French's®*
	Pinch of ground white pepper, *McCormick®*
	Salt

Prep time:	3 minutes
Cooking time:	1 minute

Preparation:

In a small saucepan, mix cream, mustard, and pepper.
Simmer until sauce thickens slightly, stirring constantly, about 1 minute.
Season to taste with salt.
Serve over pork, ham, chicken, steamed vegetables, potatoes, or rice.

Storage and Leftovers: Cover tightly and store in refrigerator for up to 2 days. Reheat in a saucepan over low heat, stirring frequently until warm.

$

MORE-THAN-MEATLOAF GRAVY

Makes 2 cups

1   tablespoon canola oil, *Wesson®*
1   tablespoon all-purpose flour, *Pillsbury®*
1   can (14-ounce) beef broth, *Swanson®*
1/4 cup tomato sauce, *Hunt's®*
1   package (1.2-ounce) brown gravy mix, *Knorr®*
     Salt and pepper

Prep time: 2 minutes
Cooking time: 8 minutes

Preparation: In a medium frying pan over medium heat, warm oil. Add flour and stir to form a paste. Let paste cook until it is a deep golden brown, about 2 minutes. Whisk in broth, tomato sauce, and gravy mix. Simmer until sauce thickens slightly, about 5 minutes. Season to taste with salt and pepper. Serve over meatloaf, meatballs, beef, veal, potatoes, or rice.

$

EASY WARM PESTO

Makes 1 3/4 cups

2   cups (packed) fresh basil leaves
1   cup pine nuts, *Diamond®*
3   tablespoons minced fresh garlic, *McCormick®*
3/4 cup shredded Parmesan cheese, *Kraft®*
3/4 cup olive oil, *Bertolli®*

Prep time: 5 minutes
Cooking time: 2 minutes (microwave)

Preparation: Place basil leaves, pine nuts, and garlic in work bowl of a food processor. Pulse until paste forms, about 1 minute. Add cheese and olive oil and pulse until mixture is smooth. Place in microwave-safe bowl. Cook on medium heat for 2 minutes or just until hot, stirring after 1 minute. Serve over chicken, veal, seafood, or pasta.

$

SHERRY MUSHROOM GRAVY

Makes 2 cups

1   can (10 3/4-ounce) cream of mushroom soup, *Campbell's®*
3/4 cup canned reduced-sodium beef broth, *Swanson®*
1/4 cup dry sherry, *Christian Brothers®*
     Salt and pepper

Prep time: 5 minutes
Cooking time: 5 minutes

Preparation: Blend soup, broth, and sherry in a blender until smooth. Transfer mixture to a heavy medium saucepan. Bring sauce to simmer over medium high heat. Stir until sauce thickens slightly, about 2 minutes. Season to taste with salt and pepper. Serve over steaks, chops, beef, turkey, or veggie burgers, omelets, potatoes, or rice.

$$

Storage and Leftovers: All the above gravies and sauces should be covered tightly and stored in refrigerator for up to 2 days. Reheat in a saucepan over low heat, stirring frequently until warm.

Clockwise from lower right: Sherry Mushroom Gravy, Easy Warm Pesto, More-Than-Meatloaf Gravy

VEGETABLE CREAM SAUCE

Makes 2 cups

1   can (10 3/4-ounce) cream of broccoli
     soup, *Campbell's*®
3/4 cup whole milk
1 1/2 cups shredded sharp cheddar cheese,
     Kraft®
2   tablespoons fresh chives, chopped
1/2 teaspoon minced fresh garlic, *McCormick*®
     Salt and pepper

Prep time: 2 minutes
Cooking time: 5 minutes

Preparation: Stir soup and milk in heavy medium saucepan over medium heat to blend. Bring to simmer. Gradually whisk in cheese and stir until melted. Stir in chives and garlic. Season to taste with salt and pepper. Serve over broccoli, asparagus, cauliflower, or potatoes.

$

RICOTTA CHIVE SAUCE

Makes 2 cups

1   can (10-ounce) cream of chicken soup,
     Campbell's®
1   cup canned chicken broth, *Swanson*®
1/2 cup ricotta cheese (or small curd cottage
     cheese)
1/4 cup fresh chives, chopped
     Pinch of ground nutmeg, *McCormick*®
     Salt and pepper

Prep Time: 5 minutes
Cooking time: 5 minutes

Preparation: In a blender, place soup, broth, ricotta cheese, chives, and nutmeg. Pulse until smooth. Transfer mixture to a medium saucepan. Stir over medium heat until sauce simmers. Season to taste with salt and pepper. Serve over noodles, rice, potatoes, or vegetables.

$

BLENDED HOLLANDAISE SAUCE

Makes 1 2/3 cups

5   egg yolks
3   tablespoons fresh lemon juice, or *ReaLemon*®
1/4 teaspoon cayenne pepper, *McCormick*®
2   sticks butter, melted, hot, *Land O'Lakes*®

Prep time: 5 minutes

Preparation: In a blender, place yolks, lemon juice, and cayenne. Pulse for 10 seconds. Add butter and pulse for 10 seconds. Serve immediately over beef, chicken, eggs, omelets, potatoes, rice, turkey, or vegetables.

$

Storage and Leftovers: All the above gravies and sauces should be covered tightly and stored in refrigerator for up to 2 days. Reheat in a saucepan over low heat, stirring frequently until warm.

Clockwise from lower right: Vegetable Cream Sauce, Ricotta Chive Sauce, Blended Hollandaise Sauce

HORSERADISH SOUR CREAM SAUCE

Makes 1 3/4 cups

1/2 cup whole milk
2 tablespoons prepared cream-style horseradish, *Silver Spring®*
1 teaspoon Dijon mustard, *French's®*
1/2 teaspoon ground white pepper, *McCormick®*
1/2 teaspoon salt
1 container (8-ounce) sour cream

Prep time: 2 minutes
Cooking time: 5 minutes

Preparation: In a medium saucepan over medium heat, stir milk, horseradish, mustard, white pepper, and salt. Simmer gently for about 5 minutes. Remove saucepan from heat. Whisk in sour cream. Serve over potatoes, vegetables, seafood, pork, or beef.

$

GARLIC CHICKEN GRAVY

Makes 1 1/2 cups

2 tablespoons butter, *Land O'Lakes®*
1 teaspoon minced fresh garlic, *McCormick®*
2 tablespoons all-purpose flour, *Pillsbury®*
1 cup whole milk
1 cup canned chicken broth, *Swanson®*
  Salt and pepper

Prep time: 3 minutes
Cooking time: 10 minutes

Preparation: In a medium frying pan over medium heat, melt butter. Add garlic and sauté 1 minute. Stir in flour to form a paste. Cook until golden brown, about 1 minute. Whisk in milk and broth. Simmer for 8 minutes until sauce thickens, whisking often. Season to taste with salt and pepper. Serve over chicken, turkey, seafood, mashed potatoes, or rice.

$

HERBED TOMATO SAUCE

Makes 2 cups

1 jar (14-ounce) tomato and basil pasta sauce, *Classico®*
2 teaspoons Italian Seasoning: Classic Herbs, *McCormick®*
1/2 cup sour cream

Prep time: 3 minutes
Cooking time: 5 minutes

Preparation: In a medium saucepan, combine pasta sauce and seasoning. Cover and cook over medium heat, stirring occasionally, about 5 minutes. Remove from heat. Whisk in sour cream. Serve over pasta, rice, vegetables, or potatoes.

$

GREEN PEPPER STEAK GRAVY

Makes 2 cups

1 tablespoon canola oil, *Wesson®*
1 cup frozen pepper strips, thawed, *C&W®*
2 cups canned beef broth, *Swanson®*
2 tablespoons all-purpose flour, *Pillsbury®*
2 teaspoons Dijon mustard, *French's®*
  Salt and pepper

Prep time: 3 minutes
Cooking time: 10 minutes

Preparation: In a medium frying pan on medium high heat, warm oil. Sauté peppers until beginning to brown, about 3 minutes. Add 1 cup broth and bring to a simmer. Place flour in a small bowl, gradually whisk in remaining 1 cup of broth until flour is dissolved. Slowly pour flour mixture into pepper mixture, whisking vigorously. Simmer until mixture thickens, stirring occasionally, about 4 minutes. Stir in mustard. Reduce heat to low and simmer for 2 minutes longer. Season sauce to taste with salt and pepper. Serve hot over beef, veal, pork, turkey, potatoes, or rice.

$

Storage and Leftovers: All the above gravies and sauces should be covered tightly and stored in refrigerator for up to 2 days. Reheat in a saucepan over low heat, stirring frequently until warm.

Clockwise from lower right: Horseradish Sour Cream Sauce, Garlic Chicken Gravy, Herbed Tomato Sauce, Green Pepper Steak Gravy

PET FOODS

Some may be wondering why I felt compelled to have a pet food chapter in this book. Since 84 percent of us feel as though our pets are our children (according to *Glamour* magazine), I thought all my pet-lover friends out there would appreciate it. My dog, Aspen, shown here enjoying a Bone-Nanza Bone, had pink paws until she was six months old (she didn't touch the ground until all her vaccinations were complete) and was the inspiration behind this chapter.

Since our pets are never with us long enough, I am always happy to indulge mine more often than not. I'm even guilty of passing table scraps when no one is looking. The following are some No-No's to remember when feeding your pets: cocoa (chocolate—dark or milk), caffeinated or carbonated anything, grapes, cherries (Aspen loves fruits), unbaked dough (yeast), beans, fat trimmings, dairy products, large quantities of fried or fast food (animals love french fries—one or two won't hurt), and foods that cause impacting such as corn kernels, dried peas, millet, etc. For more information on pet-related topics please contact me *(see page 204)*. As with children, animals need attention, supervision, and love, and as with children, they're worth every minute and more!

pet foods

pet foods

BONE-NANZA BONES

Makes 10-12 dog bones

1	jar (6-ounce) turkey and rice baby food, *Gerber®*
1/4	cup prepared savory beef gravy, *Heinz Homestyle®*
1/4	cup water
2 1/2	cups whole wheat flour, *Gold Medal®*
1	egg white

EGG WASH:
1	egg yolk mixed with 1 tablespoon whole milk

Prep time:	15 minutes
Baking time:	35-40 minutes
Cooling time:	30 minutes

Preparation: Preheat oven to 350 degrees. Line a cookie sheet with parchment or wax paper. Mix all ingredients (except egg wash) together in a large mixing bowl until a dough forms. Place dough on a floured work surface. Roll out dough to 1/2 inch thick. Using a bone-shaped cookie cutter, cut out 10-12 bones. Transfer bones to prepared cookie sheet. Brush bones with egg wash. Bake for 35-40 minutes, or until golden brown. Cool completely.

Storage and Leftovers: Store in a resealable bag in the refrigerator for up to 5 days.

$

HEALTHY HOUND STEW

Makes about 6 cups

2	cans (14 ounces each) reduced-sodium beef broth, *Swanson®*
2	tablespoons vegetable oil, *Wesson®*
1 1/2	pounds beef round steak, cut into 1-inch cubes
1/4	cup all-purpose flour, *Gold Medal®*
1	jar (4-ounce) vegetable and beef baby food, *Gerber®*
2	cups broccoli florets
1	jar (12 ounces) beef gravy, *Franco-American®*

Prep time:	15 minutes
Cooking time:	25 minutes
Cooling time:	10 minutes

Preparation: In a small saucepan, heat beef broth until boiling. Heat oil in a 5-quart pot over high heat. Add beef and cook for 3-5 minutes until browned. Using a slotted spoon, remove beef from pot and set aside. Whisk flour into juices in pot to form a paste. Slowly whisk hot beef broth into flour mixture. Bring to a boil, reduce heat and simmer for 5 minutes. Add baby food, broccoli florets, beef gravy, and beef to pot. Continue to cook for 15 minutes. Cool for 10 minutes before serving.

Storage and Leftovers: Cover tightly and store in refrigerator for up to 5 days.

$$

KITTY TUNA CAKES

Makes 35-40 one-inch button-size cakes

1	can (3-ounce) low-sodium chunk light tuna in spring water, undrained, *StarKist®*
2/3	cup dry cat food, *Purina Cat Chow®*
	Canola oil for frying, *Wesson®*

Prep time: 10 minutes
Cooking time: 10 minutes
Cooling time: 30 minutes

Preparation: Place tuna (with water) and dry food in bowl of a mini-chopper or food processor. Process until mixture is smooth and pastelike. Using a level teaspoon for each, roll mixture into 1/2-inch balls. Flatten balls into patties. Heat 1/4 inch of oil in a small skillet over medium high heat, or until oil begins to ripple. Using a metal spatula, quickly sauté the patties, about 10 at a time, for 5-10 seconds on each side, or until lightly browned. Cool before serving to your pet.

Storage and Leftovers: Cover tightly and refrigerate for up to 7 days. Do not freeze or the cakes will lose their crispness.

$

KITTY KATAFORNIA ROLLS

15-20 pieces of kitty sushi

1	package (3 ounces) smoked salmon, *Lasco®*
1/2	cup plus 3 tablespoons cooked white rice, *Minute Rice®* (no salt added)
3	tablespoons tender cat treats, *Pounce®*

Prep time: 15 minutes
Chilling time: 30 minutes

Preparation: Place smoked salmon and 1/2 cup cooked rice in a mini-chopper or food processor. Process until mixture is smooth. Place salmon mixture on a sheet of plastic wrap. Press mixture into a cigar or log about 7 inches long. Place another piece of plastic wrap on top. Using a rolling pin, flatten the mixture to 1/4 inch thick. Remove top layer of plastic wrap. Sprinkle remaining 3 tablespoons of cooked rice over pressed salmon. Replace top layer of plastic wrap and, using the palm of your hand, carefully push rice into salmon mix. Remove and discard top layer of plastic wrap. Using the bottom layer of plastic wrap as an aid, roll up the mixture (like a jelly roll) to form a log. Refrigerate for at least 30 minutes. Remove plastic wrap. Using a sharp wet knife, cut log crosswise into 1/2-inch-thick slices. Arrange pieces on a platter. Top each piece of kitty sushi with a tender cat treat.

$$

CRITTER GRANOLA

This Critter Granola is an all-in-one recipe. From bunnies to birds, all little creatures will be thankful for your thoughtful generosity and good nature in providing for their needs.

Makes 8-10 cups

1	package (3.5-ounce), unflavored microwave popcorn, popped, or 2 cups popped popcorn, *Orville Redenbacher's®*
2	cups spoon-size shredded wheat cereal, *Post®*
2	cups sunflower seeds, *Kaytee®*
2	cups rabbit pellets, *Kaytee®*
2	cups wild bird seed, *Kaytee®*

Prep time: 5 minutes

Preparation: Combine 2 cups popcorn and remaining ingredients in a large mixing bowl. Place 2 cups of granola into an outdoor-appropriate container; replenish as needed.

Storage and Leftovers: Store in airtight container at room temperature for up to 2 weeks.

$$

HEART O' SEEDS

Makes 1 heart

	Nonstick vegetable cooking spray, *PAM®*
1	cup wild birdseed, *Kaytee®*
2	egg whites, lightly beaten

Prep time: 10 minutes
Baking time: 10-15 minutes
Cooling time: 8 minutes

Preparation: Preheat oven to 325 degrees. Line a 4-inch heart-shaped metal cookie cutter with aluminum foil, allowing 2 inches of extra foil to hang over edges. Spray foil with cooking spray. Place foil-lined mold on a cookie sheet. In a mixing bowl, combine birdseed and egg whites. Pour mixture into prepared heart mold. Bake for 10-15 minutes or until firm. Allow to cool for 8 minutes. Remove heart from mold and discard foil. While still warm, use a wooden skewer to pierce a hole through the heart, approximately 1 inch from the top. Loop wire, rafia, or twine through the hole. Hang heart from your favorite tree for up to 2 weeks.

$

index

index

DEAR SEMI-HOMEMAKER,

Now is your chance to receive the *Semi-Homemade Newsletter* and *Web Magazine* <u>absolutely free</u>. Each issue is filled with new, easy how-to projects, simple lifestyle tips, and an abundance of helpful hints. Simply write to us at:

Sandra Lee Semi-Homemade
1453-A 14th Street, #126
Santa Monica, CA 90404

Or e-mail:
tips@semihomemade.com

We have received thousands of letters from our readers sharing their Semi-Homemade short-cuts, helpful hints and lifestyle tips. If you have thoughts, ideas, or suggestions please write to us at the above address. Please remember to include the following information to ensure that you'll be given appropriate credit:

Name, address, city, state, zip, area code, phone, fax, and e-mail address.

(Ideas for all areas of lifestyle are welcome: home, garden, crafts, cooking, entertaining, beauty, fashion, family, music, movies, travel, free-time activities, etc.)